THE FAMILY

HANDYMAN

DO-IT-YOURSELF

ENCYCLOPEDIA

THE FAMILY
HANDYMAN
DO-IT-YOURSELF
ENCYCLOPEDIA

*Comprehensive How-To-Series
for the entire family...
containing material from
The Illustrated
Do-It-Yourself Encyclopedia
...written in simple language with
full step-by-step instructions
and profusely illustrated*

Illustrated Edition

VOLUME
7
Fur-Guy

Published by arrangement with
Universal Publishing & Distributing
Corporation, Publisher of The
Family Handyman magazine.

ACKNOWLEDGMENTS

The editors of this series would like to express their thanks and appreciation to the following companies for their assistance in preparing special sections within this volume, for their technical advice and their permission to use special material, photographs, art and educational charts.

ADJUSTABLE CASTER CO. • ANDERSON ASSOCIATES • ARMSTRONG CORK CO. • R. BRADY CO. • CALORIC CORPORATION • CORNELL UNIVERSITY • DETROIT STEEL CORP. • DOUGLAS FIR PLYWOOD ASSOCIATION • GARDEX TOOLS • LIBBY-OWENS-FORD GLASS CO. • MASONITE CORPORATION • THE MEYERCORD COMPANY • MINNESOTA & ONTARIO PAPER CO. • MONSANTO CHEMICAL CO. • PLASTIGLIDE MANUFACTURING CO. • PPG INDUSTRIES • RAYNOR MANUFACTURING CO. • RED DEVIL TOOLS • RUBBER MANUFACTURERS ASSOCIATION • U. S. PLYWOOD CORP. • WALLBOARD TOOL CO. • WESTERN TOOL & STAMPING CO. • WOOD CONVERSION COMPANY

For their combined efforts in revising this work, the Publishers wish to thank Morton Waters, Editorial Director of THE FAMILY HANDYMAN Magazine, and Patrick O'Rourke, of Morpad, Inc., Graphic Designers.

Furniture Finishing—Adding New Surfaces

Finishing with Self-Adhesive Plastic

No doubt the fastest, easiest and surely the least messy way to get a new finish on furniture, or any other surface for that matter, is to use a material such as Con-Tact. Most dime and department stores sell it as do some hardware stores. Con-Tact, or one of the other brands, has a self-adhesive back covered by paper until ready for use. It is easily cut with an ordinary pair of scissors and will adhere well to flat dry surfaces.

This is a quick way to obtain an attractive, durable finish. There is no need for paste, tacks or nails. The material is resistant to stains, scratches and scuff-marks. And it's very easily cleaned with a damp cloth.

This finishing material is available in wood grains, marbles, unusual patterns and solid colors. It will stick to almost any clean, dry surface, such as plywood, metal, painted plaster, glass, wallpaper, plastic and tile. Available in 18" wide rolls, it is cut to shape with a pair of scissors.

A raw plywood table top is being given a rich wood-grain finish by rolling on self-adhesive vinyl.

Before—a flat-grained piece of furniture which has little grace or charm.

After—the rich wood-grain plastic covering enhances the beauty of this cabinet.

Transfers for a New Finish

It's possible to reclaim old furniture or to give new furniture an exciting look with special transfers available in wood grains, marble and leather. This paper-thin material is exceedingly rugged and has been used industrially for many years. It can be used not only on furniture but also on kitchen cabinets to add the warmth of wood.

Cut the plastic transfer with a razor and a straight edge, preferably one made of metal.

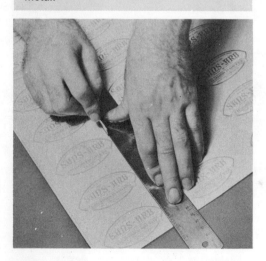

Apply a special adhesive to the surface of the cabinet. This cement will provide the necessary bond for the plastic veneer.

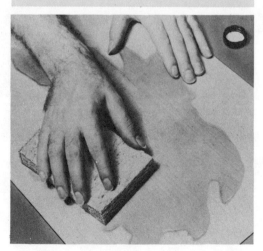

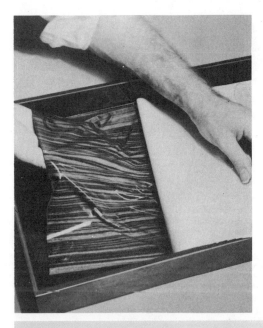

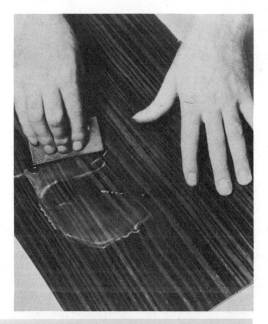

Soak the cut piece of plastic in water for several minutes until the protective coating slides off easily. This coating covers the printed side of the transfer.

Lay the plastic transfer in place on the cabinet and smooth with a squeegee, usually supplied with the material and adhesive when you purchase it.

This material is just as easy to apply to vertical surfaces as to horizontal surfaces. Always cut the material to exact size before you soak it to remove the protective covering.

Here the panel insert of the door is being covered. Always work the squeegee from the center outward toward the edges of the material. This will remove any air bubbles between the plastic sheet and the wood surface being covered.

Photographs courtesy of The Meyercord Co.

Furniture Plans

Although power tools make the job easier, there are many handymen who prefer to make their furniture with hand tools. Unless you are fairly skilled with tools, you will find that contemporary pieces are the simplest to make. Most cutting is along a straight line and corner joint construction is kept simple. On the other hand, period furniture involves intricate cutting and shaping, and some of the work cannot be done without a lathe and other power tools.

In the plans on the following pages, you will find some simple and some involved projects. Every plan can be modified to meet your requirements and your skills. Should you wish to make changes, re-read the basic primer section and make modifications accordingly.

But before you start on any project, remember that good furniture making involves:

1. accurate and careful workmanship

2. use of good woods and attractive grains, unless the pieces are to be painted

3. proper finishing—this cannot be rushed if you wish to obtain a craftsmanlike result.

Collect your tools, materials, plans and . . . good luck!

Planter-Coffee Table

This attractive coffee table, 24″ by 48″, is made of fir plywood and rests on four ¾″ hardwood dowel legs. It is easy to make with ordinary hand tools.

The tools you need are: rule, square, hand saw, center punch, drill, bits, countersink bit, brace and

Materials Needed

1 Top	24"x48"	¾" plywood
2 Side aprons—Part C	3⅝"x50"	¾" hardwood
2 End apron—Part A	3⅝"x24"	¾" hardwood
2 Cleats—Part D	¾"x48"	¾" hardwood
4 Legs—Part B	¾" hardwood dowels 15" long	

No. 10 flat and round head screws, 1¼" long; sandpaper

screwdriver bit, expansion bit or jig saw, keyhole saw or coping saw.

Follow the accompanying step-by-step instructions and you'll be able to make this unusual planter-coffee table in a single evening.

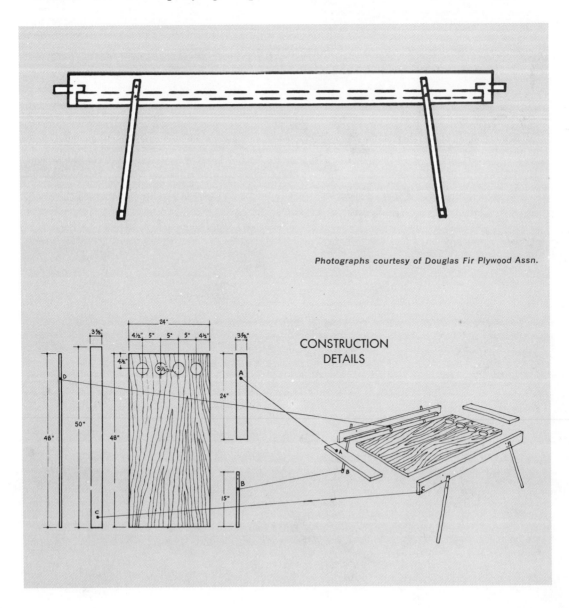

Photographs courtesy of Douglas Fir Plywood Assn.

CONSTRUCTION
DETAILS

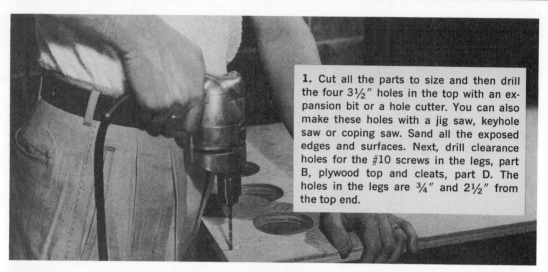

1. Cut all the parts to size and then drill the four 3½" holes in the top with an expansion bit or a hole cutter. You can also make these holes with a jig saw, keyhole saw or coping saw. Sand all the exposed edges and surfaces. Next, drill clearance holes for the #10 screws in the legs, part B, plywood top and cleats, part D. The holes in the legs are ¾" and 2½" from the top end.

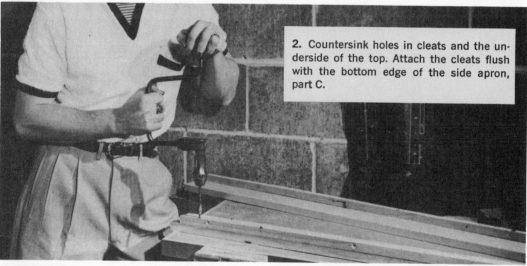

2. Countersink holes in cleats and the underside of the top. Attach the cleats flush with the bottom edge of the side apron, part C.

3. With the end apron, part A, lapped 1" over the edge of the top, drill ⅝" deep pilot holes in bottom side to correspond to clearance holes. Fasten apron in place.

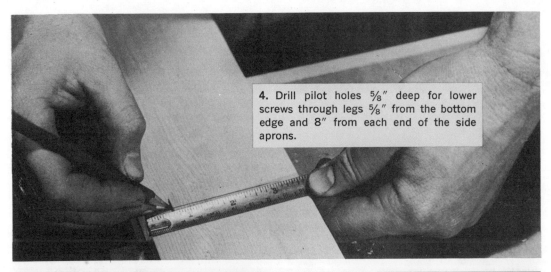

4. Drill pilot holes ⅝" deep for lower screws through legs ⅝" from the bottom edge and 8" from each end of the side aprons.

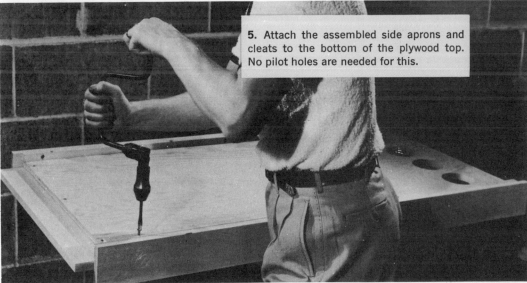

5. Attach the assembled side aprons and cleats to the bottom of the plywood top. No pilot holes are needed for this.

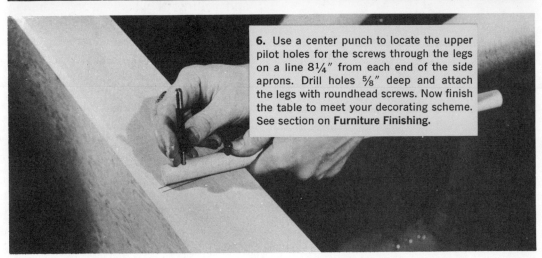

6. Use a center punch to locate the upper pilot holes for the screws through the legs on a line 8¼" from each end of the side aprons. Drill holes ⅝" deep and attach the legs with roundhead screws. Now finish the table to meet your decorating scheme. See section on **Furniture Finishing**.

Photograph courtesy of Rubber
Manufacturers' Association

Basic construction plans for table.

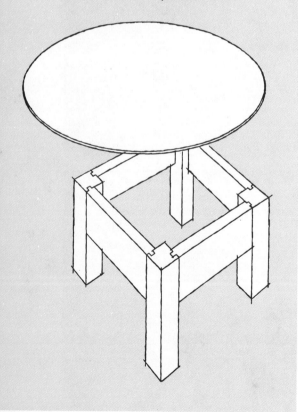

Play Table for Children's Room

If you have an old table about and want to convert it to a play table for your youngsters, or you'd like to build one from scrap, here's a novel idea. Use rubber tiles over the surface and band the edge with an aluminum or chrome metal trim.

The resulting play table is as durable as it is attractive. Pounding and rolling of wheels won't damage the rubber, which also helps to muffle the sound of energetic play activities. Crayon marks, paint and ink are easily cleaned from the rubber tile surface.

If you wish to make this table from scratch, make the top out of ¾″ plywood cut in circle form, 36″ to 48″ in diameter. The top rests on a base made of 2x2 wooden legs and a frame of 1x4's so that the top is 14″ above the floor. See *FURNITURE—BASIC PRIMER* for leg joint details.

End or Bedside Table

This unusual table with a glass top and lower storage compartment can be built with ½″ pipe legs or with attractive plywood legs. It is easy to make out of ¾″ fir plywood, a 44″ strip of ¼″x1″ hardwood and a piece of plate glass 24″x25½″.

The only tools you need are: a hand saw, rule, square, hammer, center punch, nail set, drill, bit and screwdriver.

Follow the step-by-step instructions and you'll find that you can make this table in a few hours.

1. Cut all the parts to size as noted in the materials list. Sand all surfaces and edges. Then glue and nail the bottom and shelf, part E, to the plywood back.

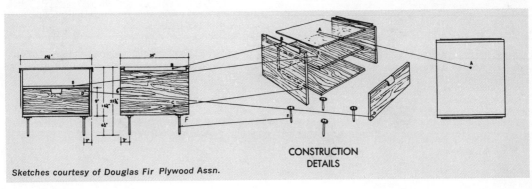

CONSTRUCTION DETAILS

Sketches courtesy of Douglas Fir Plywood Assn.

2. Set the hardwood retaining strips, part B, so that they project ¼″ past the top edge of the sides, part C. Secure in place with glue and brads.

3. Next, glue and nail the sides so that they line up with the front edges of the shelf and bottom pieces. Set nails and brads; fill holes before finishing.

4. Fit the door in place between the bottom and the shelf. Center-punch to locate the holes for the hinges in the bottom and then attach the door with a piano hinge.

5. Drill a hole for a friction or bullet catch into the top edge of the door. Drive the catch into place. The handle is made of a piece of leather 3″ wide and 5″ long.

6. If you wish to use pipe legs, attach pipe flanges 3″ from front, sides and back by drilling holes for screws. To protect the floors, insert dowels into the bottom opening of the pipes so that the dowels project about ⅛″. For other types of legs, see leg construction details which follow. Now sand all surfaces and finish.

Materials Needed

1 Plate glass top—Part A	¼"x24"x25½"	
2 Retaining strips—Part B	1 "x22"	¾" hardwood
2 Sides—Part C	16 "x24"	¾" plywood
1 Door—Part D	8 "x24"	¾" plywood
1 Back	8¼"x24"	¾" plywood
1 Shelf—Part E	24 "x24"	¾" plywood
1 Bottom	24 "x24"	¾" plywood

1 piano hinge 24" long, with screws; 4 Pipe legs ½"x6½", with flanges and screws; I Friction catch; 6d finishing nails; brads; glue; sandpaper.

Leg Details

There are several different types of legs you can use with this piece of furniture as well as others shown in this section. These legs can be made of ¾" plywood or, if you wish, 1" hardwood stock.

Note the accompanying illustrations showing the leg details. Cut the parts to size indicated, smooth all surfaces and edges. You can use the plywood edge tape, if you wish, or fill the end grain and paint the entire leg—black blends in well with contemporary furniture.

Handles You Can Make

While you can purchase any of a large variety of handles in a hardware store or lumber yard, there are many unusual handles you can make yourself. Here are just a few; maybe these will spark your own ideas.

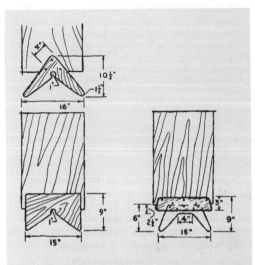

Alternate leg details.

Leather handle is made of a piece 3" wide and 5" long. Glue one end around a dowel, ½" in diameter. To attach the handle, you can cut a slot in the door or drawer front or else notch out a piece 3" wide and ⅛" deep. The back of the leather is fastened with glue and small round-head screws.

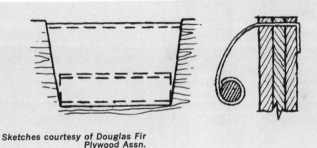

Sketches courtesy of Douglas Fir Plywood Assn.

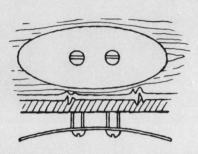

A piece of elliptically shaped brass can be fastened with bolts through thin brass tubing to make a modern pull. Smooth all metal edges and use brass bolts or paint the bolt heads black.

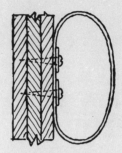

A piece of leather, 3″ wide and 9″ long, can be shaped into a loop to act as a drawer or door pull. Two roundhead screws with washers directly beneath the heads fasten leather to drawer or door.

A wooden ball, available in many sizes in specialty lumber yards, makes an attractive pull. A screw is countersunk in the wooden ball to hold it fast to the forward surface of the door or drawer. Wooden balls are also available in hardware stores; these use a bolt to fasten in place.

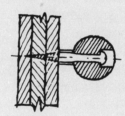

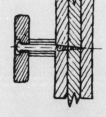

Wooden trim and moldings also make unusual pulls. Here are two types which can be used when making furniture.

Make Your Own Ping-Pong Table

Here is a ping-pong table which is a welcome addition in any recreation room. Because of its simple construction and assembly, it can be taken apart and stored in a small space. It can also be taken outdoors and used on the patio or terrace in warm weather.

If you don't go in for ping-pong, you can make this table for general utility about the home. It is very handy as an extra serving table both indoors and outdoors.

All you need is a single piece of ¾″ plywood, 5′ by 9′, or you can make the top out of two pieces, 60″ x 54″ joined with a piano hinge on the underside. For the base, you need a 4′x8′ sheet of ¾″ or ⅝″ plywood.

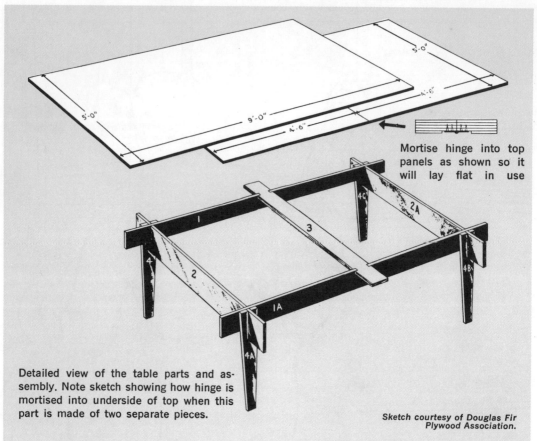

Mortise hinge into top panels as shown so it will lay flat in use

Detailed view of the table parts and assembly. Note sketch showing how hinge is mortised into underside of top when this part is made of two separate pieces.

Sketch courtesy of Douglas Fir Plywood Association.

Layout of table frame parts showing how they can be cut out of a single 4'x8' sheet of ¾" or ⅝" plywood.

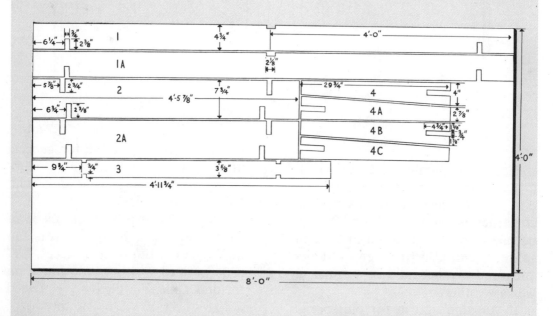

Cutting How-To

1. The top may be made from one piece—a 5'x9' plywood panel—or two pieces 5'x4' 6" hinged in the center. A hinged top, of course, will require less storage space. If you hinge the top, see hinge detail diagram.

2. The pieces for the base may be cut from one 4'x8' panel (as shown) or from one 8'x30" panel.

3. On one of your panels, carefully mark the frame pieces to dimensions shown in the diagram, and cut them with a sharp handsaw or power equipment, if available.

4. The notches in the various panels should be accurate in width. They can easily be made by drilling a hole at the bottom line and sawing each edge into the hole. The corners can be trimmed with a chisel.

5. Sand all edges. You are now ready to finish the table.

Finishing How-To

1. Apply two coats of exterior enamel undercoater. The initial or prime coat is important; for this coat it is recommended that the undercoater be thinned in the proportions of one quart of pure linseed oil per gallon of paint.

2. Brush on one coat of exterior enamel in any color desired. Green is recommended for a ping-pong table.

3. Be sure to paint the underside of the top with one or more coats of the undercoater.

4. Seal all edges with undercoats and finish coat. For best results in finishing, sand lightly between finish coats.

For General Use Inside

1. For a light stain finish to retain natural beauty of wood, apply a resin sealer, followed by a stain coat, then a flat or gloss varnish as a wearing surface.

2. Seal the underside of the top with one or more coats of the resin sealer.

3. Finish all edges with sealer and other coats.

Alternate Interior Finish

1. Apply coat of interior undercoater, followed by a coat of interior paint.

2. Apply one or more coats of the undercoater to the underside of the top.

3. Finish all edges with undercoater and finish coat.

For Ping-Pong Table

1. The ping-pong table top should be painted in dark green color, in a flat, thin, nonreflecting paint.

2. One procedure for achieving such surface would be to apply a coat of lacquer sanding sealer, followed by a flat green pigmented lacquer. Edges would be finished, of course, and the underside of the top should have one or more coats of the sanding sealer or other protective coating.

ASSEMBLY—The base may now be assembled as pictured in the sketch. The simple lock joints hold the base rigid without the use of any fastenings. It may be readily taken apart and stored until needed again.

Drop-Leaf Table-Cart

This ingeniously designed serving table-cart can be used as a buffet table, a tea table, movable bar or a dining table for two. When not in use, it adds a decorative note as a side table in a finely furnished room.

As planned here by designer Russel Wright, power tools are needed to cut the miters and grooves. The setting of the blind dowels calls for a certain amount of skill. However, these plans can be modified if desired—just re-read the basic primer section and you will find easier ways to do the same job.

No matter which method you choose for the construction, you will be able to build a beautiful and useful table of which you and your family will be proud. As designed by Mr. Wright for the series of Famous Designer Plans, the table is made of Weldwood African Mahogany plywood with legs of solid mahogany and a drawer bottom of green Mi-

Photograph courtesy of United States Plywood Corp.

carta or laminated plastic. You can, of course, use any other hardwood-veneered plywood you like.

Here are the basic plans together with the materials you will need to make this striking table-cart.

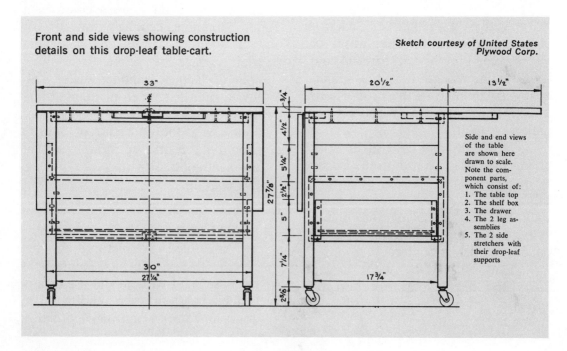

Front and side views showing construction details on this drop-leaf table-cart.

Sketch courtesy of United States Plywood Corp.

Side and end views of the table are shown here drawn to scale. Note the component parts, which consist of:
1. The table top
2. The shelf box
3. The drawer
4. The 2 leg assemblies
5. The 2 side stretchers with their drop-leaf supports

Materials Needed

TOP	1 center 33"x20½"x¾" plywood good-2-sides 2 leaves 33"x13½"x¾" plywood good-2-sides
LEGS, SHELF BOX, AND FRAME	4 legs 24⅝"x1⅜" solid mahogany 2 side stretchers 27¼"x1⅜"x⅜" solid mahogany 2 end stretchers 17¾"x1⅜"x¾" solid mahogany 2 side panels 27¼"x9"x¾" plywood good-2-sides 2 end panels 17¾"x5⅜"x¾" plywood good-2-sides 1 shelf 28½"x19¼"x¾" plywood good-2-sides 2 drop-leaf supports 14⅞"x3"x¾" plywood 2 drawer-slides 27¼"x1⅜"x½" maple or other very hard wood 1 center tie 17¾"x2"x1" maple or other very hard wood
DRAWER	2 sides 28½"x5"x¾" plywood 2 ends 17⅝"x5"x¾" plywood 1 bottom 29"x16⅝" ¹/₁₆" Micarta bonded to ⅛" hardboard
OTHER MATERIALS	4 4" hinges with ⅝" screws to fit 4 Bassick casters No. 9439-SC-RP with clear plastic wheels 2¼" carriage bolts, 1¾" long, with nuts and flat washers Presto-Set glue Mahogany veneering strips for edges 1 qt. Satinlac, wood filler, sandpaper, and fine steel wool (00) Contact Cement.

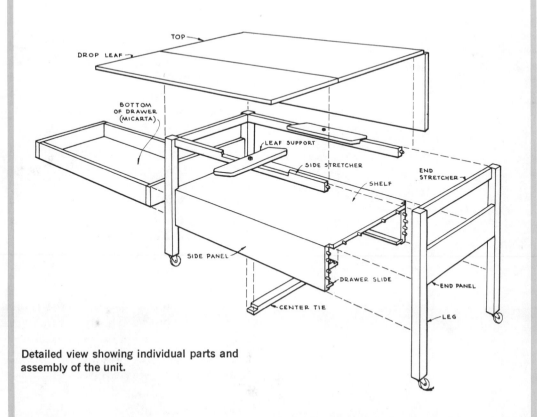

Detailed view showing individual parts and
assembly of the unit.

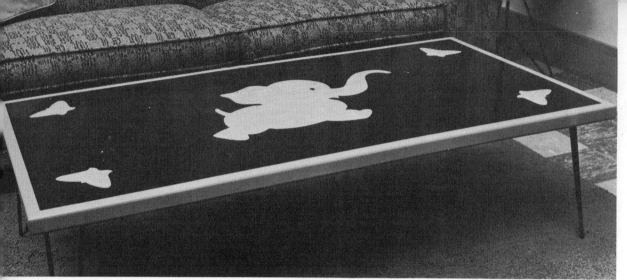

Pink Elephant Coffee Table

This rubber-topped coffee or cocktail table with a pink elephant and butterfly inserts should be a special inspiration for a weekend project because resilient rubber is easy to cut into any pattern. Furthermore, the rubber top is easy to clean and won't be harmed by spilled drinks.

Make the base for the table out of a piece of ¾″ plywood and attach two cleats, out of 1x4, to the underside about 1″ from the ends of the table. Use #9 flathead screws 1½″ long, and blue, to fasten cleats.

The edge around the table is mitered out of hardwood stock, ½″ x1½″, and attached with glue and 6d finishing nails. Counterset the nail heads. Note that this edging should extend above the top of the plywood so that the rubber top is flush with the top of this trim.

The wrought iron legs are screwed into the 1x4 cleats at each corner of the table.

Cut the rubber inserts for the table as well as the rubber top. You can use roll goods or tiles, whichever is more convenient. Cement the rubber to the top of the plywood.

After the rubber surface has dried in place, sand all wooden edges and apply a finish.

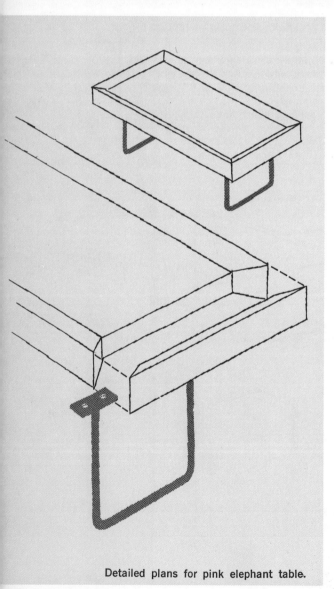

Detailed plans for pink elephant table.

Materials Needed

4'x4' ¾" plywood panel (choice of wood up to you)
1 pair of 3" hinges for the butterfly supports
2 pairs of 2" hinges for the drop leaves
6 1" angle irons for attaching the table top
16 ¾" No. 6 flathead wood screws for the 2" hinges
12 ¾" No. 8 flathead wood screws for the 3" hinges
12 ¾" No. 6 roundhead wood screws for the 1" angle irons
40 2" No. 10 flathead wood screws for shelf and legs
8 1½" finishing nails
Plastic resin glue
¹⁄₁₆" Micarta panel 30"x60"
1 qt. contact cement and applicator
1 qt. Satinlac
Fine steel wool (Number 00)
Furniture paste wax
Spackle and oil color for making Swedish putty—or wood veneer for edge banding
4 "Domes of Silence"

Drop-Leaf Coffee Table

You needn't have an elaborate workshop to make this striking coffee table. The shelf provides convenient storage and the two hinged sides lift up to provide additional surface space when needed.

It was designed by Freda Diamond out of rift oak plywood and topped with black Micarta.

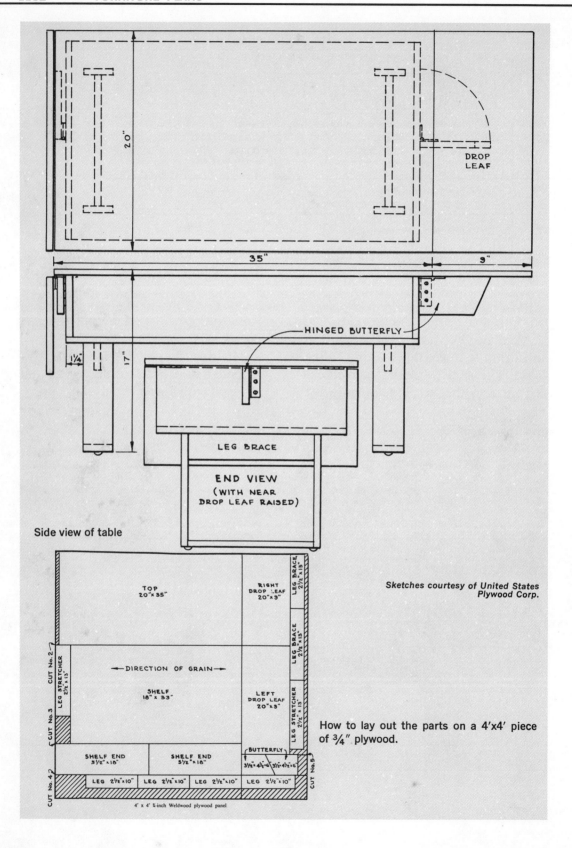

DROP LEAF

35"

9"

2 0"

HINGED BUTTERFLY

1¼"

17"

LEG BRACE

END VIEW
(WITH NEAR
DROP LEAF RAISED)

Side view of table

TOP
20"x35"

RIGHT
DROP LEAF
20"x9"

LEG BRACE
2½"x13"

CUT No. 2

←DIRECTION OF GRAIN→

LEG STRETCHER
2½"x13"

CUT No. 3

LEG BRACE
2½"x13"

SHELF
18"x33"

LEFT
DROP LEAF
20"x9"

LEG STRETCHER
2½"x13"

SHELF END
5½"x18"

SHELF END
5½"x18"

BUTTERFLY
3½"x4¼"x6" 3½"x4½"x6"

CUT No. 4

LEG 2½"x10"   LEG 2½"x10"   LEG 2½"x10"   LEG 2½"x10"

CUT No. 5

4' x 4' ¾-inch Weldwood plywood panel

Sketches courtesy of United States
Plywood Corp.

How to lay out the parts on a 4'x4' piece
of ¾" plywood.

Stacking Cabinets

Here's a novel and sensible idea in the way of cabinets. These stacking cabinets of fir plywood are finished in bright decorator colors. Used separately or stacked on top of one another, they fit into almost any room in the house.

To make the cabinets:

1. Cut the top and bottom out of ¾" plywood to size—11¾"x23".

2. Cut dadoes or grooves for sliding doors as shown in the detail sketch. You can use the alternate technique with ¼" quarter-round and ¼" square stock or any of the methods shown in the basic primer:

3. Drill four holes, ½" in diameter, through bottom and top for legs.

4. Cut two sides out of ¾" plywood to size—11¾"x11¾".

5. Cut two doors out of ¼" plywood to size—11⅝"x10⅝". Drill finger-grip holes as shown in sketch. These holes are 1" in diameter.

6. Rabbet the top and bottom edges of the sides to receive top and bottom of the cabinet.

7. Cut four legs out of ½" hardwood dowel; each should be 15⅞" long.

8. Cut back panel out of ¼" plywood to size—11"x23".

To assemble the unit, it is necessary to sand all edges and surfaces smooth and then:

1. Glue and nail one side to the top, bottom and back.

2. Insert two of the legs and fasten to the side as shown in the detail sketch using a #8 roundhead screws 1" long.

3. Slide doors into grooves.

4. Attach the other side to the top, bottom and back with glue and nails.

5. Slip the other two legs through the pre-drilled holes and fasten the side.

Materials Needed
EACH CABINET
Top, bottom and ends: 2'x3', ¾" plywood
Back, sliding doors: 2'x2', ¼" plywood
Legs: 5½' of ½" dia. hardwood dowel rod
1 Doz. 1" No. 8 roundhead wood screws; glue; 4d, 6d finishing nails
(if alternate door detail is followed); door guides: 8' of ¼" quarter-round; door guides: 4' of ¼" square stock.

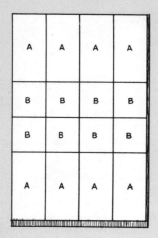

¾"x4'-0"x6'0" PLYPANEL A-D (MATERIAL FOR 4 CABINETS)

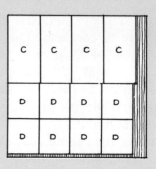

¼"x4'-0"x4'-0" PLYPANEL A-D (MATERIAL FOR 4 CABINETS)

How to cut the basic parts for four cabinets out of 1 sheet of 4'x6' plywood ¾" thick and a 4'x4' sheet of ¼" plywood. Part A is top and bottom, 11¾"x23"— part B the sides, 11¾"x11¾"—part C the back, 11"x23"—and part D the sliding doors, 10⅝"x11⅝".

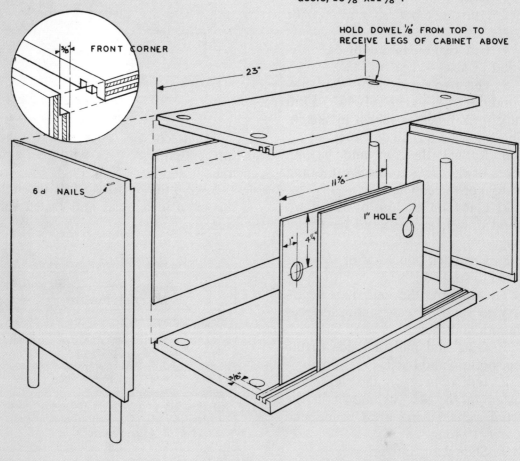

HOLD DOWEL ⅛" FROM TOP TO RECEIVE LEGS OF CABINET ABOVE

FRONT CORNER

6 d NAILS

23"

11⅜"

1" HOLE

1"

4¼"

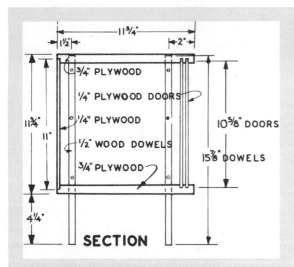

Sectional or end view of the cabinet.

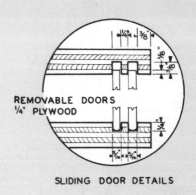

SLIDING DOOR DETAILS

Details for cutting grooves for the sliding doors in the top and bottom of the cabinet.

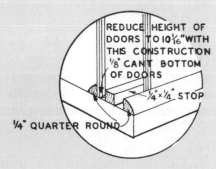

ALTERNATE DOOR DETAIL

Alternate plan for making sliding doors.

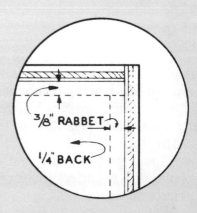

BACK CORNER DETAIL

Details for joining back.

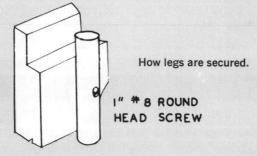

How legs are secured.

Sketches courtesy of Douglas Fir Plywood Association.

Buffet Storage Chest

Simplified contemporary design has created this striking combination buffet and storage unit which is made of fir plywood and painted iron legs. The slope-front drawers are ideal for storing linens and flatware and the top of the unit is perfect for serving light buffet meals.

For this unit you will need a 24"x30" piece of ¼" plywood, one 4'x4' and one 4'x8' panel of ⅜" plywood and one piece of ¾" plywood 48"x54", plus 2½' of 2x4, 2½' of 1x2 and 38" of ⅝" steel rod.

1. Cut the parts as noted in the accompanying material list and shown in the detail sketches.

2. Fasten the drawer guides to the inside surface of the two sides of the chest. Use glue and 1" brads for the job.

3. Attach the divider guide to the underside of the top of the chest as shown in the accompanying sketch.

4. Set the base between the two sides and secure in place with glue and 6d finishing nails, countersinking the heads. Fasten the top as well in the same manner.

5. Set the back panel into position with glue and brads.

MAKING THE DRAWER

These unusual drawers are easy to make and can be used in any piece of furniture you design as well as this buffet storage chest. Here's how to cut and assemble a sloping front drawer:

1. Cut the bottom out of ⅜" plywood to size—28⅜" wide and 22⅞" deep.

2. Cut two sides out of ⅜" plywood to size—3" high and 20⅞" long. Next, cut the bevel on the front of each side as shown in the sketch; the top of the side piece is 19⅞" long and the bottom is 20⅞" long.

3. Cut the back for the drawer out of ⅜" plywood to size—3" high and 26¾" long.

4. The drawer front is cut out of ¾" plywood; it is 4"x28⅜". The top and bottom edges are bevel cut with a saw or plane as shown in detailed sketch. Next, cut a rabbet along each edge—13/16" wide and ¼" deep.

5. Set the back between the two sides and join with glue and 1" brads, forming butt joints at each corner.

6. Place the sides and back on the drawer base so that the back is 2" from the rear edge of the base and a 7/16" space is left on each

side. Fasten in place with glue and 1″ brads.

7. The front of the drawer is mounted last. It is fastened with glue and 6d finishing nails into the sides and the base of the drawer.

8. Sand all edges smooth so that the drawer slides freely back and forth on the guides attached to the sides.

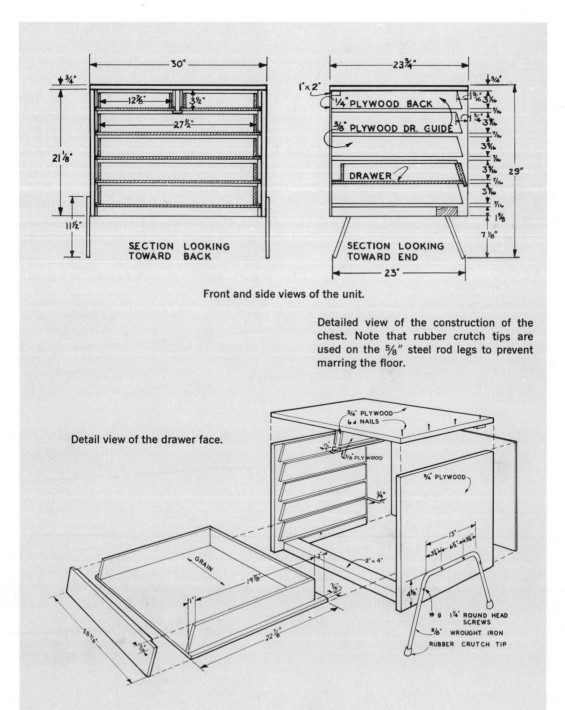

Front and side views of the unit.

Detailed view of the construction of the chest. Note that rubber crutch tips are used on the 5/8″ steel rod legs to prevent marring the floor.

Detail view of the drawer face.

Base and Wall Cabinets

These attractive units can be built individually as separate wall and base cabinets or used in pairs as shown in the accompanying photograph. These were designed by Norman Cherner to be cut without waste from standard-size plywood panels.

It is best to use glue with another type of fastener—screws or nails—to make secure joints. You will find C-clamps or hand screws valuable in holding parts together while the adhesive is drying.

The units shown here have painted metal handles. It is possible to use any type of handle you find that fits into your decorating scheme. For additional handles, as well as leg con-

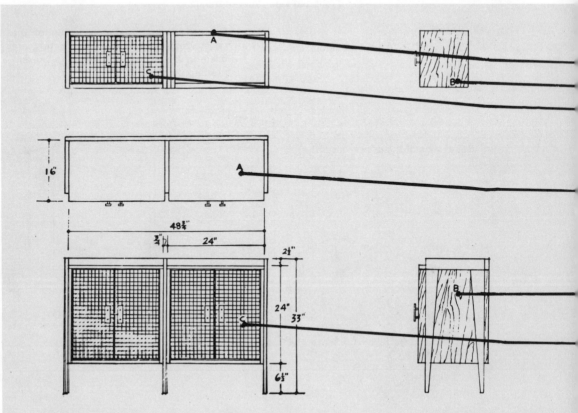

Materials Needed

BASE CABINET

1 Top (A)	16"x24"	¾" plywood
1 Back	22½"x22½"	¾" plywood
2 Sides (B)	16"x23¼"	¾" plywood
1 Bottom	16"x22½"	¾" plywood
2 Doors (C)	11"x22¼"	¾" plywood
Legs	¾"x4"x14'	fir, pine or hardwood
2 Side aprons	¾"x3¼"x14"	fir, pine or hardwood
1 Back apron	¾"x2½"x50¼"	fir, pine or hardwood, if cabi-

nets are built in pairs; if only one cabinet is constructed, back apron is 25½" long.

2 handles; 2 piano hinges 22" long, with screws; 2 friction catches; 6d finishing nails, screws, glue, sandpaper; 4 furniture glides ½"size.

HANGING CABINETS

1 Top (A)	12"x24"	¾" plywood
1 Back	12½"x24"	¾" plywood
1 Bottom	12"x24"	¾" plywood
2 Ends (B)	12"x14"	¾" plywood
2 Doors (C)	11¾"x12¼"	¾" plywood
1 Spacer	12"x14"	¾" plywood

2 handles; 2 piano hinges 12" long, with screws; 2 friction catches; 6d finishing nails, glue, sandpaper.

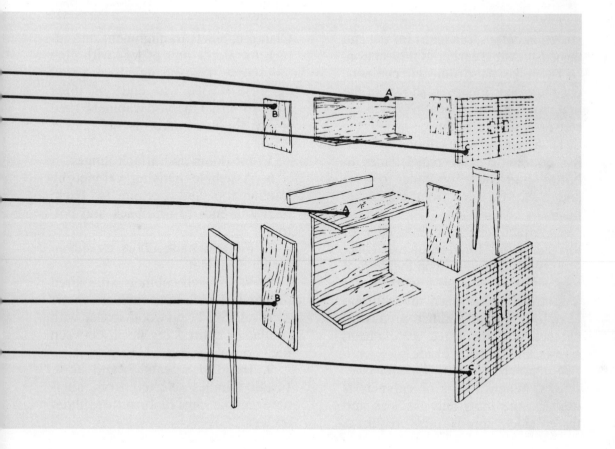

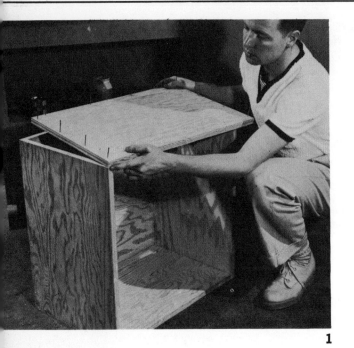

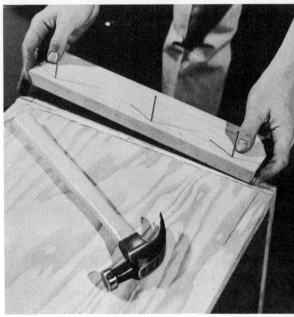

1   2

struction details, see plans for the end or bedside table earlier in this section.

To make these unusual cabinets, cut the pieces to size as shown in the materials list and follow this step-by-step assembly procedure:

1. Assemble base cabinet by nailing bottom to back panel; sides to bottom and back; top panel to sides and back. Be sure front edges are flush.

2. Attach side aprons to edge of top panel, ¾″ forward of rear edge.

3. With pencil, outline location of legs with tapered edge toward center and straight edge lined up with end of apron. Within outlined area, drill cabinet side for three #9 flathead screws. Countersink inside.

4. Attach legs with glue and 1¼″ screws. When a pair of cabinets is used as one unit, only six legs and three side aprons are required.

Clamp cabinets in alignment and attach to middle pair of legs with glue and screws. Fasten single back apron ¾″x2½″x50¼″ to ends of three side aprons. On base cabinets used singly, the back apron is ¾″x2½″x 25½″.

5. Fit doors and attach hinges.

6. Assemble hanging cabinet by joining top and bottom to back; then join ends to top, back and bottom.

7. Fit and hang doors as shown for base cabinet.

8. When wall cabinets are paired to match double base cabinets, insert a ¾″x12″x12″ plywood spacer with similar or contrasting finish between the two wall units.

9. Install door catches and stops. Install handles selected from alternate details. Install furniture glides on legs.

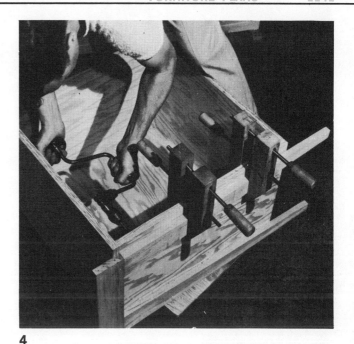

3 **4**

5 **6**

This combination unit, made of walnut plywood and black Micarta, is used for the bar top and for alternate leaves of the screen. It is a high-style furniture piece designed by Edward Wormley.

Unusual Screen-Bar

Edward Wormley, one of the great innovators in contemporary furniture design designed this screen-bar as a high-style piece of furniture. The bar stands 6′ high and it may be used from the front or rear. When not in use, it is covered by a handsome screen made of alternate panels of hardwood-veneered Weldwood plywood and Micarta. It can be made of other woods, of course.

The bar is designed with built-in lights that cast a soft glow down on the stemmed glasses which hang from racks on each side of the bar. As planned here, the bar requires five 6′ brass piano hinges which run the full length of the screen. They are especially attractive when light is reflected from the long brass strips, but for economy's sake, you may prefer to use a less expensive hinge technique. You can substitute several butt hinges, but decide upon which one you like and can afford before cutting the parts.

Here are the basic working drawings together with a materials list. The more advanced handyman can build this unit from these plans following the techniques of construction given in the basic primer and elsewhere in this section.

Materials Needed

- 2 4'x6'3/4" plywood panels (good-2-sides)
- 1 4'x6'3/4" plywood panel (good-1-side)
- 1 4'x8'1/16" Micarta
- 3 1/4"x1/2"x4'6" solid stock for the drawer and glass racks
- 1/4"x1/2"x10'6" solid hardwood for drawer slides and glass frame
- 12"x12"x1/8" hardboard panel
- 10 5/8"x34 3/8"x1/8" white flash opalescent glass
- 2 20" 60-watt Lumiline lamps with 4 mounts
- 1 1/2" toggle switch
- 10' of No. 16 insulated wire
- 5 6'x1 1/4" (open) continuous brass hinge
- 1 3'x1 1/4" (open) continuous brass hinge
- 2 gross 5/8" No. 5 oval-head brass screws
- 1 gross 1/2" No. 5 oval-head brass screws
- 50' of 1/8"x3/4" edge banding or wood veneer
- 14 single-pin 3/4" "Domes of Silence"
- 2 quarts Satinlac
- 8 1/4" adjustable shelf pins
- 3' 1/4" dowels
- 3' 3/8" dowels
- 1/2 gross 1 1/4" No. 10 flathead wood screws
- 2 polished brass pulls for drawer and door
- 1 magnetic door catch

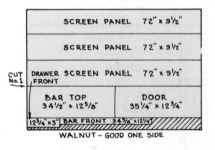

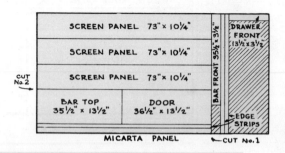

Plans for cutting the basic parts out of plywood and plastic laminate.

Front and side views of the screen-bar.

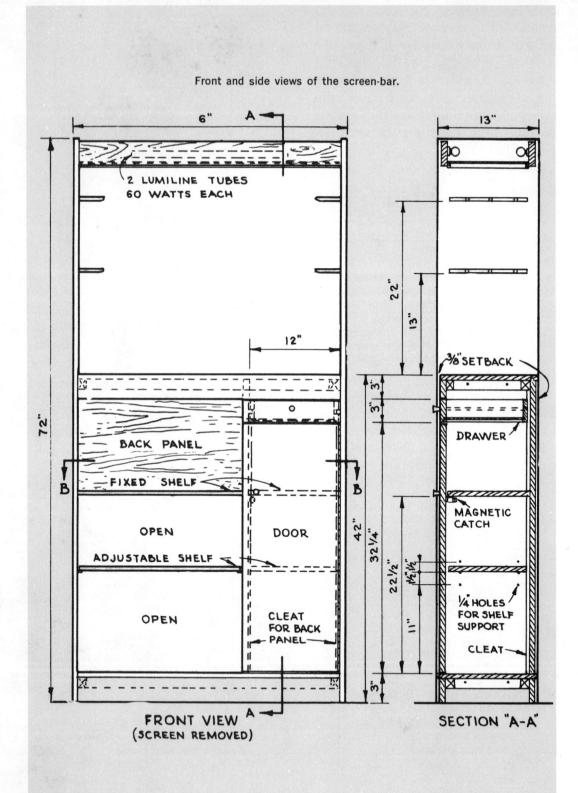

FRONT VIEW
(SCREEN REMOVED)

SECTION "A-A"

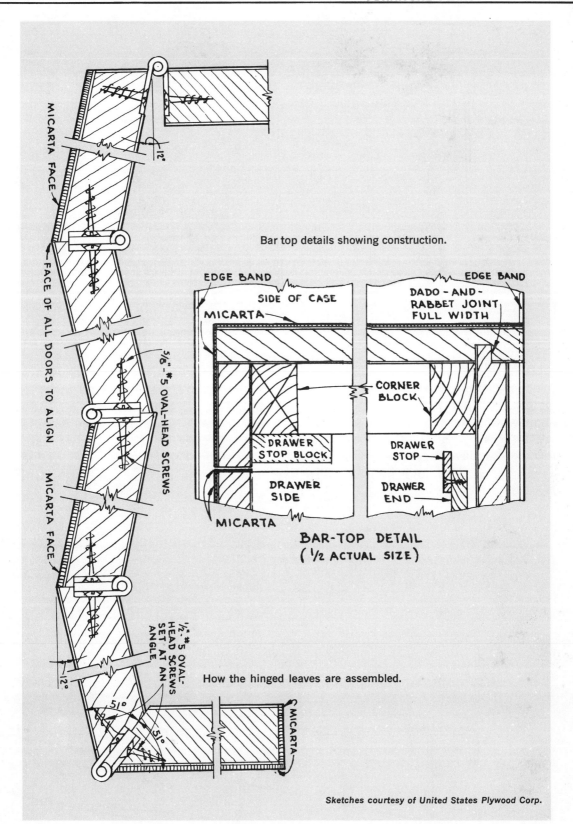

MICARTA FACE

FACE OF ALL DOORS TO ALIGN

MICARTA FACE

5/8"-#5 OVAL-HEAD SCREWS

12°

Bar top details showing construction.

EDGE BAND

SIDE OF CASE

MICARTA

EDGE BAND

DADO - AND -
RABBET JOINT
FULL WIDTH

CORNER
BLOCK

DRAWER
STOP BLOCK

DRAWER
STOP

DRAWER
SIDE

DRAWER
END

MICARTA

BAR-TOP DETAIL
(1/2 ACTUAL SIZE)

1/2" #5 OVAL-
HEAD SCREWS
SET AT AN
ANGLE

12°

51°

51°

How the hinged leaves are assembled.

MICARTA

Contemporary Desk

This attractive contemporary desk is made of fir plywood and pieces of hardwood and pine. There are several types of legs and drawer pulls which can be used; see earlier suggestions on legs and pulls in this section.

To make the unit, cut all parts as noted in the materials list. Sand all edges and surfaces smooth and you're ready to assemble the unit. Remember, all joints, except for the center apron and leg rails, are glued and nailed.

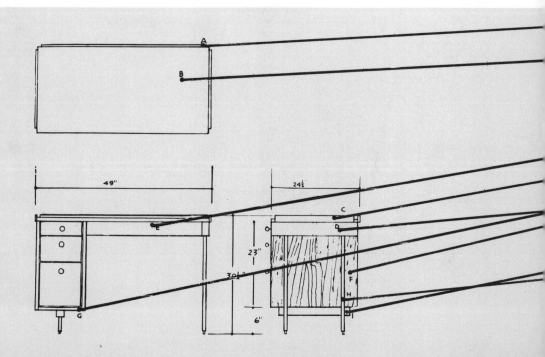

Materials Needed	1 Back strip (A)	1½"x46"	½" hardwood
	1 Top (B)	2'x4'	¾" plywood
	2 Side strips (C)	1½"x22"	½" hardwood
	1 Leg rail (D)	3⅝"x24"	1⅝" fir or pine
	1 Leg rail (I)	2"x20"	1⅝" fir or pine
	1 Center apron (E)	3⅝"x32¾"	1" fir, pine or hardwood
	1 Cabinet bottom (G)	12"x24"	¾" plywood
	2 Cabinet sides (F)	23"x24"	¾" plywood
	1 Cabinet back	12"x22¼"	¾" plywood
	2 Legs (H)	¾"x29"	Steel pipe (not threaded)
	2 Legs (J)	¾"x6"	Steel pipe (not threaded)
TOP DRAWER:	1 Front	3⅝"x11⅞"	¾" plywood
	1 Back	2⅜"x10⅞"	¾" plywood
	2 Sides	2⅜"x22"	½" plywood
CENTER DRAWER:	1 Front	6⅜"x11⅞"	¾" plywood
	1 Back	5⅛"x10⅞"	¾" plywood
	2 Sides	5⅛"x22"	½" plywood
BOTTOM DRAWER:	1 Front	12"x11⅞"	¾" plywood
	1 Back	10¾"x10⅞"	¾" plywood
	2 Sides	10¾"x22"	½" plywood
	3 Drawer bottoms	11⅞"x22"	½" plywood
	6 Runner strips	¾"x¾"x22"	plywood, pine or hardwood

3 drawer handles; 4 angle braces 2", with screws; 4 crutch tips, or hardwood dowels, for ends of legs; 9 flathead wood screws; 2½" and 3½" brads; 6d and 4d finishing nails; glue; sandpaper.

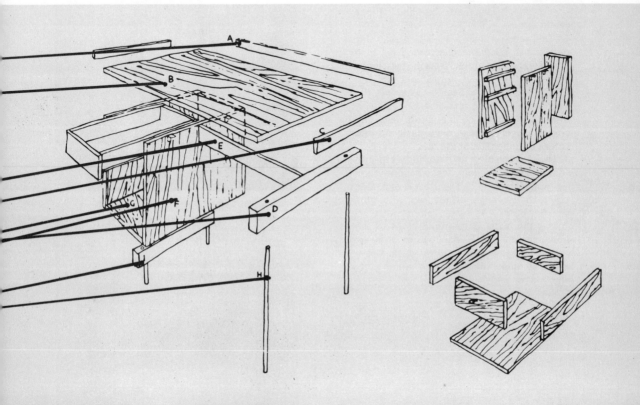

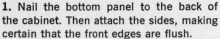

1. Nail the bottom panel to the back of the cabinet. Then attach the sides, making certain that the front edges are flush.

2. Measure down $2\frac{15}{16}''$, $9\frac{3}{8}''$ and $21\frac{7}{16}''$ from the top edge of the cabinet to locate the upper surface of each of the three drawer runners on each side. Exactly $\frac{1}{16}''$ clearance is left above and below each drawer front. The ends of the runners, $\frac{3}{4}''$ from the forward edge of the cabinet, act as drawer stops.

3. Drive pipe legs into tight holes drilled into leg rails. Drill and countersink cabinet bottom on centerline for three #9 flathead screws $2\frac{1}{2}''$ long. Fasten the rail with glue and screws. Drill the cabinet side and countersink inside for two #9 flathead screws $2\frac{1}{2}''$ long into the end of the center apron.

4. Drill and countersink $1\frac{5}{8}''$x$3\frac{5}{8}''$ leg rail for two #9 flathead screws $3\frac{1}{2}''$ long into the center apron. Attach two angle braces to the side of the cabinet and two to the leg rail. It is best to assemble the desk upside down on a bench or floor. After the cabinet, center apron, legs and angles are assembled, slide desk top into braces to underside of the top.

5. Use 6d finishing nails through top into edges of the cabinet, center apron and leg rail. Attach $\frac{1}{2}''$x$1\frac{1}{2}''$ back and side strips to the edge of the top with glue and 1" brads. Assemble all drawers by joining the back, bottom and sides to the front panel. Attach handles to drawers and set them in place in the desk. Counterset all nail heads, fill with wood putty and you're ready to finish the unit.

Photographs courtesy of Douglas Fir Plywood Assn.

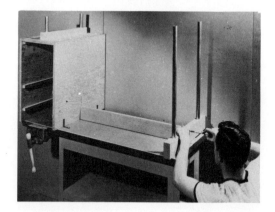

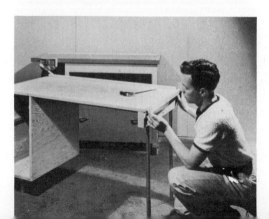

Photograph courtesy of United States
Plywood Corp.

Decorative Storage Chest

Peter Hunt, probably the outstanding American authority on decorative peasant art, has designed this handsome storage chest which has dozens of purposes around the house. It can serve as a window or fireside seat and is readily moveable for it has easy-rolling ball-casters in each leg.

It is easy to construct and the painted decorations can be applied even by those who have had no previous experience in doing such work. This chest was made of maple plywood but you can use any type of wood you wish.

Although the plans for this decorative chest were prepared by Mr. Hunt for distribution by United States Plywood Corporation and its dealers, here is a complete list of materials and working drawings for the more advanced handyman to follow.

Materials Needed

4'x8'¾" lumber core plywood
4'x4'⅜" Novoply panel
48—1½" No. 10 flathead steel screws
12—1⅛" No. 10 flathead steel screws
4—¾" ball-casters
1 box 1" finishing brads
Presto-Set glue
36' ½"x¾" No. 8432 pine parting strips (for nailing strips)
10' ¾" No. 8610 flat screen molding
10' 1¹⁄₁₆x3½" No. F402 clam-shell base molding
10' ⁷⁄₁₆"x1¹⁄₁₆" No. 8422 shoe molding
2 black hammered butt-strap hinges, with ¾" wide butts
1 slotted brass stay hinge for lid
2' ⅜" dowels for screw-hole plugs
4—1½" No. 6 flathead steel screws for hinge butts
2 good-grade camel's-hair brushes Nos. 10 and 11
4 tubes of oil colors—red, green, blue, yellow, and white
½ pint turpentine
½ pint clear varnish
paste wax
Satinlac

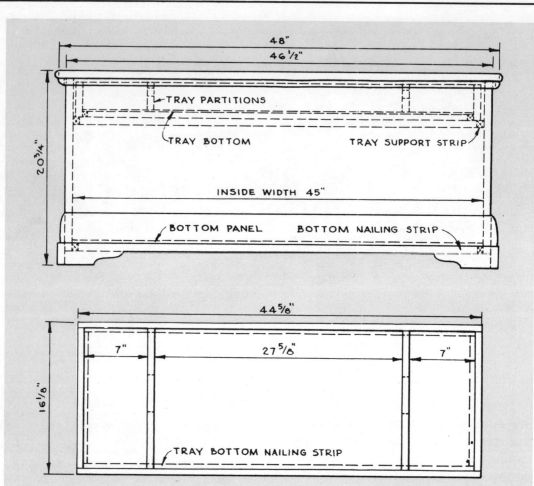

Front and side views of the chest plus a top view showing basic dimensions and assembly of parts

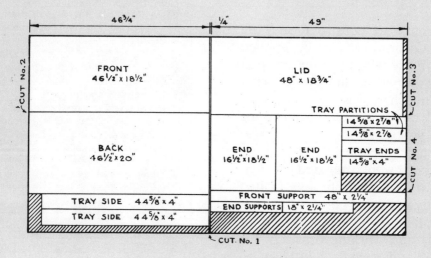

How to lay out the pieces for cutting.

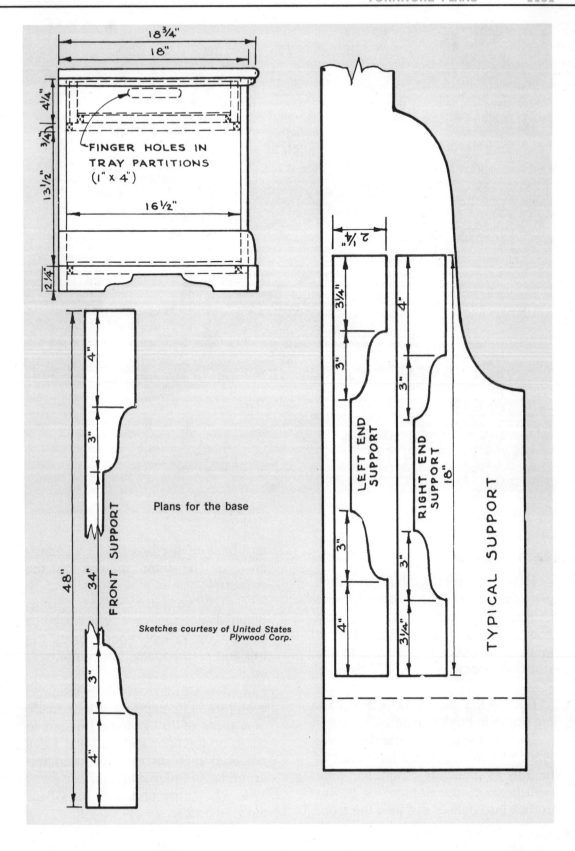

18¾"

18"

FINGER HOLES IN
TRAY PARTITIONS
(1" x 4")

16½"

4¼"
¾"
13½"
2¼"

4"

3"

FRONT SUPPORT

48"

34"

3"

4"

Plans for the base

*Sketches courtesy of United States
Plywood Corp.*

2¼"

3¾"

3"

4"

3"

LEFT END
SUPPORT

3"

4"

3"

RIGHT END
SUPPORT

18"

3¾"

TYPICAL SUPPORT

Photograph courtesy of United States Plywood Corp.

Twin Bunk Beds

Here is a furniture built-in which provides two beds in a room for two children and yet makes the most floor space available. Each bed is made as a unit and fastened to the studs in the wall with 4″ flathead screws.

Here is the basic how-to for making this twin bunk bed unit:

1. The frames for the beds are made of 1x6's with butt joint corners held by #9 flathead screws 2½″ long with heads countersunk. Two braces are set into dadoes cut into the front and back of the bed frame and fastened in the same manner as the corners.

2. You can use No-Sag springs under a mattress or else set a piece of ⅜″ or ½″ plywood across the top and rest a foam rubber mattress on it.

3. The storage cabinet is made as a built-in. The exposed side is made of a piece of ½″ plywood nailed to cleats on the floor and wall and 1x2's are used to form the sides and top around a ¾″ plywood door.

4. The entire unit rests on a base made of 1x2's.

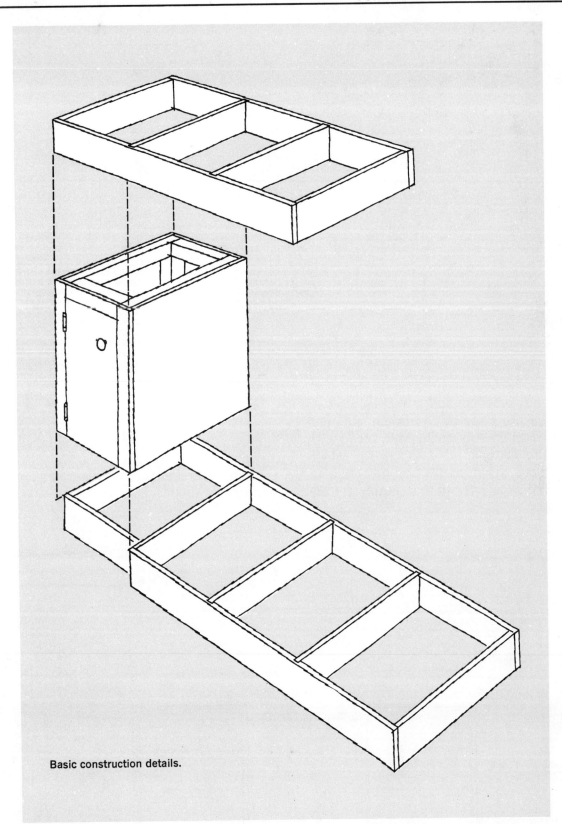

Basic construction details.

Vanity Chest

A practical and attractive piece of furniture for any bedroom, this plywood chest is designed to blend with the bedside table, plans for which were given earlier in this section. You can refer to that section for additional plans for drawer pulls and leg details.

It is also recommended that you refer to the *basic primer* for another technique of hinging the lift up counter section holding the make-up mirror.

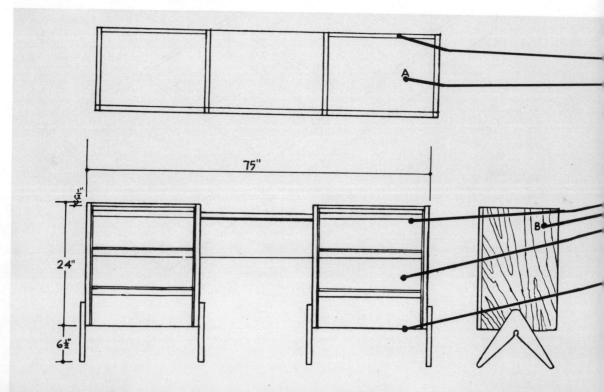

Materials Needed

ONE CHEST ONLY

1 Top (A)	16"x24"	3/4" plywood
2 Sides (B)	16"x24"	3/4" plywood
1 Bottom	14"x24"	3/4" plywood
1 Back	22 3/4"x24"	3/4" plywood
3 Drawer fronts	7 1/2"x23 7/8"	3/4" plywood
6 Drawer sides	6 1/2"x14 1/4"	3/4" plywood
3 Drawer backs	6 1/2"x22 3/8"	3/4" plywood
3 Drawer bottoms	14 1/2"x23 7/8"	3/4" plywood
4 Drawer runners	3/4"x3/4"x14"	fir, pine or hardwood
3 Facing strips	3/4"x3/4"x24"	fir, pine or hardwood
1 Facing strip	1/2"x3/4"x24"	fir, pine or hardwood
2 Retaining strips for drawer bottoms	1/2"x1/2"x20"	fir, pine or hardwood

4 Furniture glides, 1/2" sizes
6d and 4d finishing nails, screws, glue, sandpaper.

VANITY

1 Top	16"x24"	3/4" plywood
1 Front	7 5/8"x24"	3/4" plywood
2 Sides	6 7/8"x15 1/4"	3/4" plywood
1 Back	6 7/8"x22 1/2"	3/4" plywood
1 Bottom	15 1/4"x24"	3/4" plywood
1 Facing strip	3/4"x3/4"x24"	fir, pine or hardwood
1 Piano hinge	24" long, with screws	
1 Mirror	14"x22", with clips or glue to fasten to underside of top.	

6d and 4d finishing nails, screws, glue, sandpaper.

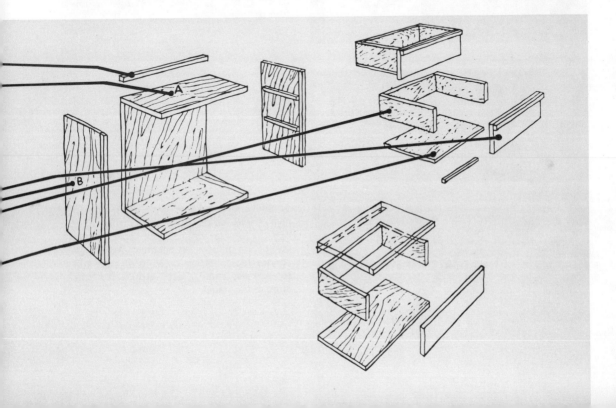

Photographs courtesy of Douglas Fir Plywood Assn.

1. Nail back of chest to bottom. Be sure edges align perfectly.

2. After sides are attached flush with back and bottom panels, install top by nailing first through top into back and then through sides into top. (Sides project ½″ past top and ¾″ past front edge of bottom panel.)

3. Screw two runners onto each side to give three equal spaces (a trifle over 6¹³⁄₁₆″) for drawers. (Bottom drawer slides on bottom panel—not runners.) Apply ¾″ square facing strips to edge of side and top panels, and ½″x¾″ strip along rear edge of top panel.

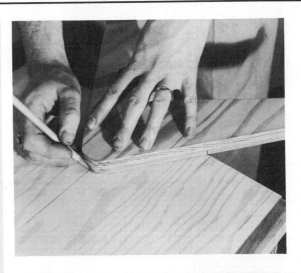

4. On leg edges, mark location of chest bottom 6½" from floor and outline leg location centered on chest. Drill side panel on centerline 1" below apex of leg for No. 9 flathead screw. Countersink inside.

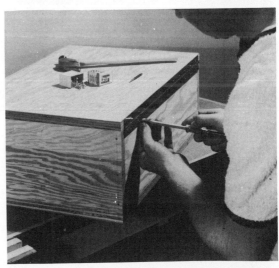

5. Assemble vanity sections by nailing two sides to back; bottom to sides and back; and front to sides and bottom. Attach hinges to top and back panel. Apply facing strip to forward edge of top.

6. Construct drawers by nailing sides to back; front to sides; and bottom panel to sides and back. Upper edge of drawer front lines up with upper edges of sides. On the top and center drawers, ½" square strips prevent thin ¼" drawer bottoms from sagging. (Do not add to lower drawer; the chest bottom supports drawer and strip would keep it from closing.) After painting, suspend vanity between chest sections by driving two No. 9 flathead screws 1¼" long in each side. Mirror may be attached to underside of top with clips or glue.

Furniture Repairs, Glued

Furniture usually comes apart because of dampness in the atmosphere or in the wood itself; because moisture gets into the joints when the piece is washed and this dissolves the glue; because in a dry, hot atmosphere, the wood shrinks and the glue dries out; or because some part is not plumb with the rest of the piece, or does not fit properly, and the strain breaks the glue.

The parts to be reglued will hold together only when they are completely free from the old glue, paint, and other surface covering; when the wood is dry and the pores are open; when the parts to be glued are close-fitting, with all surfaces touching each other; and when they are held together tightly until dry (about 1 to 24 hours, depending upon the type of glue).

Tools and Supplies

Select from the following list what you need for your own gluing job.

Glue—Most glues are good but many are not moisture resistant and few are waterproof. The urea resin glues that come in powder form to be mixed with water are strong and moisture resistant, and do not dry speedily. Cements of various type are not as a rule so strong as woodworking glues. Other furniture glues which you can use include casein, white polyvinyl liquid (which does not stain and generally won't mar the surface finish), as well as hide and fish glues. For absolutely waterproof gluing, a resorcinol resin glue is best, but it is also excellent for ordinary furniture repairs because it fills gaps successfully, which most glues won't do.

Clamps—Several clamps of different sizes to hold glued parts together. If you cannot get clamps, use:

Rope to hold large joints together; a new clothesline is good.

Cord to hold small joints together; heavy fish line or sash cord is good.

Spikes, clothespins, or round 5″ sticks; these are to use with rope or cord to make tourniquets.

Large rubber bands cut from an old inner tube.

Vise.

Claw hammer.

Hard-rubber tip to put over the end of the claw hammer; tips used on the end of canes or crutches will serve. A piece of leather over a wood mallet or a paper pad may be used instead.

Brace and bit, or hand-drill and

straight-shank drills for making holes in wood.

Coping saw or other small saw.

Sharp jackknife.

Sandbag—In size about 5"x8", and three-fourths full of dry sand.

Board—In size about 1"x8"x12" to use on top of sandbag.

Dowel sticks to replace missing or broken rungs or old rungs.

Dowel pins—Spiral or grooved pins, from 3/8" to 5/8" in size, to mend dowel joints.

Sandpaper—Medium and coarse.

Newspaper—These keep the table clean and make good pads to use under clamps or rope.

Shears to cut paper and cloth.

Rags to wipe off the glue.

Vinegar to wash off hide or liquid fish glue.

Small stick of soft wood to make wedges.

Preparation for Gluing

Sometimes a part of a piece of furniture may have been put in the wrong way or in the wrong place; it may crack, break, or pull apart.

To prevent this mistake, mark the parts of each loose joint with the same numbers or letters before they are taken apart, so they may be put together again quickly and in the same places. Then pull all the loose pieces apart.

Those that do not pull out easily, gently knock apart by tapping with the rubber-tipped claw hammer. Do not force them, or some part may crack or break.

Most joints that are already tight may be left that way; when it is necessary to open a tight joint, try working hot vinegar into it to dissolve the glue; this will work if hide glue was originally used, which is likely to be true in the case of old furniture.

Be sure all the old glue is entirely cleaned off. Gently scrape or chip off the thickest parts, being careful not to remove any wood. Then wash off with hot vinegar every bit of glue that remains; this quickly dissolves hide glue without injuring the finish.

Open the pores of the wood to allow the glue to enter freely, either by dipping the parts to be glued in warm water and letting them dry thoroughly, or by laying them on top of a warm radiator or stove, or in the sunshine until they are warm.

When the parts are clean and thoroughly dry, put all of them together again to test them for proper fit. If they fit closely, they are ready to be glued. If an end that goes into a hole fits a little loosely, then glue

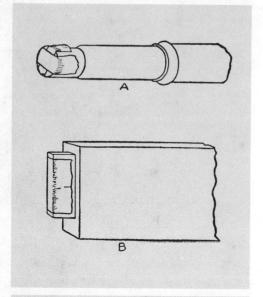

Strips of soft, cotton cloth, if glued over ends a little small for holes, will make a tight joint.

one or two strips of cotton cloth over the end until it fits snugly into the hole or use a gap-filling glue such as resorcinol resin or casein; or glue in a dowel or a piece of wood the right size and shape and, when it is dry, bore a new hole in it of the correct size. This is always done when the hole is much too large.

Gluing Parts Together

Have all materials, tools, and glue laid out ready to use. Lay all parts in place as they are to be reassembled, having numbers or letters matching. That is, for a chair, lay the right legs and rungs at the right side of the seat, the left ones at the left side, the front pieces in front, and the back ones behind the seat.

Because some glues set quickly, the parts of the furniture to be glued should be in place and braced before the glue sets.

Have the furniture and the glue at room temperature if the room is warm, because cold wood and cold glue, except casein glue, may not hold well. Rub the glue well into the pores of the wood with a stiff brush, covering all surfaces to be joined, and press the pieces in place. Freshly glued pieces should be held tightly together until the glue has set hard. Of the various types and sizes of clamps, select the ones that force the parts together the best. If clamps cannot be had, use a rope or a stout cord and with a spike or round stick make a tourniquet to draw and hold the parts closely together. Always protect the wood and finish from damage by using soft wood pieces or thick pads of paper under clamps or the ropes where they touch the furniture.

Immediately after all of the parts have been glued and clamped, wipe the glue from the finish while it is still soft. Use a stick cut to a smooth chisel-edge to clean around the joints and small places, and then wipe the rest of the surface with a clean damp cloth. Let the piece remain until the glue is dry (about 24 hours unless a fast-setting glue has been used). See *ADHESIVES*.

How To Clamp or Tie Joints Together

Find in which direction pressure is needed before putting on the clamps or rope. Always put the greatest pressure right on or near the parts being glued together. Have the clamps or tied ropes directly over or near the joint or break, to draw the pieces close together and to hold them there until the glue has dried.

Sometimes it is necessary to use two clamps or to tie two pieces of rope, one on either side of the part being glued, to get enough pressure to draw the parts together. To hold the rung tight, place the clamp on the legs directly over the place where the rung enters; or if rope is used, pass it around the two legs at the point where the rung enters. If a rung is being glued on the other side of the chair at the same time, place a second clamp or rope in the same way.

When a loose chair back or the top of a chair is being glued, pass one end of the rope down the front and under the seat and tie it to the other end that comes over and down the back. Make the tourniquet at the front of the chair. Two ropes, one at each side of the back and tied in the same way, are better than one. If the two ropes slip off the top of the back after they are tied, hold them together with the cord.

Dowel Joints

A dowel or pin that holds a furniture leg in place sometimes breaks, leaving one or both ends in the holes. Bore the dowel out of the hole with a brace and bit, or a hand drill with straight-shank drills slightly smaller than the diameter of the dowel. Never bore beyond the depth of the dowel because the hole may become too deep or the bit in some cases may go through to the other side. Usually you can tell when to stop because boring through the hardwood dowel is slower than bor-

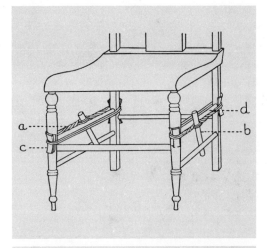

A rope and tourniquet hold the glued parts together: a, rope; b, tourniquet; c, pad to prevent marring; d, glued rung.

Sketch from Cornell Extension Bulletin #684, "How To Glue Furniture" by Charlotte Brenan Robinson.

ing through the soft wood of the furniture. With a small chisel or penknife, chip and force out what remains of the dowel, but do not cut the hole any larger. Wash out the glue with vinegar. Then select a new dowel that fits the hole snugly.

Dowels with spiral or straight grooves are best because they let the air and excess glue come out as the dowel is put in place. If the parts of the joint do not come close together, the dowel may be too long. Cut a piece off the end of the pin, round the cut with a sharp knife or sandpaper, then follow the directions for gluing.

Dowel Sticks for Chair Rungs

If an old rung of the same size as the broken or missing one cannot be found, a dowel stick may be used to replace the broken rung. Select one of the same diameter as that of the rungs already on the chair. To get the length, measure the distance between the legs and add the depth of the two holes into which the dowel stick will be glued; then cut it off. At each end of the new rung make pencil lines completely around the stick to mark the depth of the holes. With a sharp knife cut straight down and deep into the pencil lines. Put the rung into a vise with one end toward you. With a sharp knife, or a chisel and hammer, and working away from you, shave the dowel, cutting straight back from the end to the deep cut, then test to see whether it is the right size for the hole. Keep cutting all the way around if necessary, until the end fits the hole snugly. Then trim the other end of the dowel. Round off both ends slightly with a sharp knife or with coarse sandpaper. If the end is long for the depth of the hole, cut a little piece off and round the end again. Clean all old glue out of holes in the legs with warm vinegar; glue the new rung in place as directed.

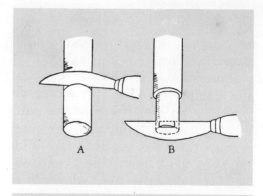

Cutting the ends of a new dowel. A, cut around the dowel on the pencil line; B, shave the end of the dowel to fit the hole snugly; cut away from you with a knife or a chisel and hammer.

If an ornamental turned rung is missing, sometimes a similar one of the right length can be purchased at a second-hand shop.

Simple Breaks

Simple breaks on legs, rungs, spindles, and arms that are diagonal or lengthwise of the piece may be glued; those broken straight across the short way or across the grain, and table tops, need special tools and skill to repair them.

A new break may be ready to glue and brace together immediately. An old break that has been glued before, must first be washed out to remove the glue and then reglued as directed.

Because there is likely to be great strain where the back legs are fastened to a chair seat, those places may need to be made more secure. After the glue has dried, put a long slim screw through the leg and the seat. Countersink this screw, cover the head with matching wood or water putty, and paint it, or apply matching shellac stick, so that the place will not show.

Small Cracks

Cracks such as those at the ends of table leaves can be glued. Gently force the crack open with several small wedge-shaped pieces of soft wood. With a hammer gently tap the point of the wedges into the crack, one at a time, beginning at the edge of the leaf, until the crack is opened far enough to receive the glue. Be careful not to split the crack farther. Work the glue in with a slim stick or small brush. Remove the wedges and clamp the crack together tightly.

Veneer

Small pieces of loose veneer and blisters may be glued in place. Lay the loose piece of veneer face down on a flat surface and scrape off the glue. Do not wet the veneer. Then apply the glue to the furniture but not to the veneer. Lay the veneer in place, add a paper pad, and clamp it down, or lay the sandbag on top

of it. Be sure the bag covers and holds in place all parts of the piece of veneer. If necessary, put a flat board, with weights on it, on top of the sandbag.

With the point of a sharp knife, cut a slit at the side of the blister where the veneer is still glued. Be sure to follow the grain of the wood. Hold the slit open with the knife, fill the blister with warm vinegar, and let it stand for several hours to dissolve the glue. Remove any vinegar that remains, and let the blister and the surrounding wood dry thoroughly before adding glue. Then work plenty of glue under the blister and clamp it down or lay the sandbag on it. If the sandbag is not heavy enough to hold the veneer flat, put a board with a weight on top to hold it down.

Chips and Small Pieces

Chips and small pieces can be treated like loose pieces of veneer, but the glue should be brushed on both the chip and the place where it goes.

Furniture Upholstery Repairs

Upholstered furniture consists basically of a frame, strip or cleat webbing, padding, and cover. Some furniture also has spring upholstery. Repairs needed on upholstered furniture generally include recovering, replacement or redistribution of padding, replacement or refastening of webbing, and regluing, reinforcing, or replacing frame parts. With spring construction, replacing, anchoring, and retying springs may also be necessary. Loose cushions may also

be repaired; for this information refer to the section *CUSHIONS, INNERSPRING.*

Recovering

Replace the entire cover if the covers on seat, back, or arms are torn, soiled, or worn beyond repair.

Even with fairly new furniture it is usually impossible to match new material to worn or faded fabric, so all sections must usually be recovered when one is damaged.

Procedures for recovering upholstered furniture vary with furniture design, but the following general procedure applies to almost all types:

1. Remove old cover carefully, taking out all tacks.

2. Using the old cover as a pattern, cut a piece of new material to approximate shape and size.

3. Smooth out and replace any lumpy or torn padding and lay new cover in place, making certain all four sides have the same amount of surplus material.

4. Tack center of opposite sides, stretching the material lightly but firmly. Do not drive tacks all the way in. Work from center to edges, stretching material evenly. If wrinkles develop, remove tacks and work the wrinkles out. Note how the old covering was folded and fitted at corners and around legs and arms. If this was satisfactory, fit the new cover the same way. When covering fits smoothly, drive tacks all the way in.

5. After covering is tacked to the side of the frame, cover tack heads with an edging or gimp. Fasten gimp with large-headed upholstery nails spaced about 2″ apart.

Replacement or Redistribution of Padding

Padding of tow, cotton batting, excelsior, or moss is used over the

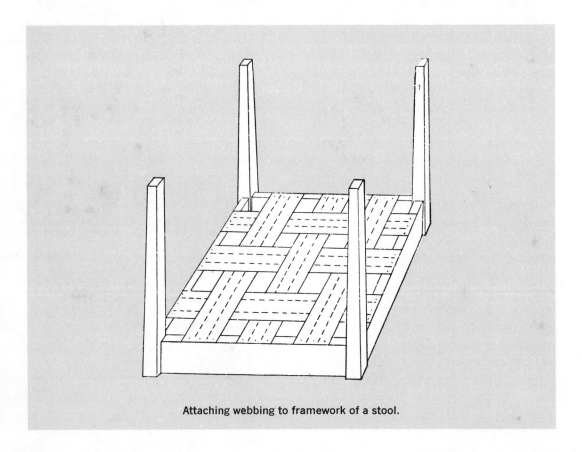

Attaching webbing to framework of a stool.

springs in the case of spring construction, or on the webbing in the case of padded construction. When padding shifts or becomes lumpy, remove the cover and redistribute or replace the padding. To replace padding:

1. First, remove all old padding and tack a piece of burlap smoothly over the entire surface to be padded.

2. Spread padding evenly over the burlap, forming a compact cushion about 1½″ thick.

3. Cover this with a second piece of burlap or muslin, tacked down securely, and place a 2″ layer of cotton batting on top. Pull off surplus cotton around the edges; do not cut the cotton since this will make a ridge under the cover.

4. Tack a cambric cover over the frame bottom to keep padding from working through to springs or webbing and falling out.

5. Replace cover as described previously.

Repairing Frame

Tighten loose frame joints with glue blocks, pins and screws, or angle irons. Repair any frame damage.

Repairing Webbing

Check strip or cleat webbing for signs of wear or breakage whenever cover is removed. Replace damaged webbing and refasten loose strips. To insure that webbing will hold securely, double it over at the ends to give tacks more gripping power, tighten, and tack so stress is at right angles to tack length. Run webbing in two directions, at right angles to each other. Closing the entire bottom with webbing is not necessary, but too much webbing is better than too

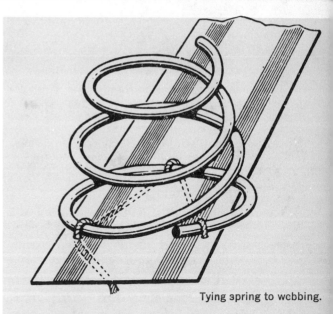

Tying spring to webbing.

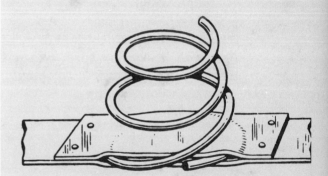

Fastening spring to metal strip.

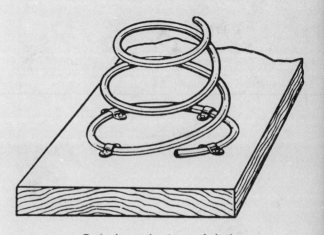

Fastening spring to wood cleat.

little. If springs are to be anchored to webbing, space the webbing to support spring bases. Similarly, anchor metal strips or wood cleats securely and space them for springs.

Adjusting Springs

Springs may shift, bend, or become damaged otherwise. Re-anchor and retie loose springs; replace those that are damaged.

Springs are usually attached differently on webbing, on metal strips, or on wood cleats. Fasten spring bases to webbing with heavy flax cord about ⅛" in diameter. Anchor springs to metal strips with clamps. If clamps loosen, rivet them. Fasten springs to wood cleats with staples or metal straps and nails.

After springs are anchored, retie them with heavy flax cord like that used to anchor springs to webbing:

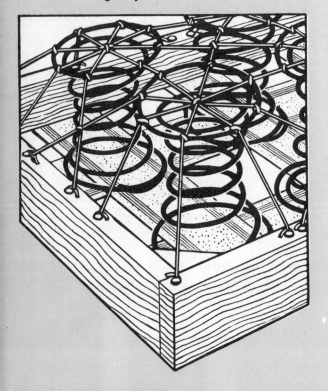

Springs tied lengthwise, crosswise, and diagonally.

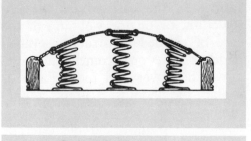

Springs tied in place.

1. Nail cord to the center of one side of the frame. Pull it over the top of the springs to an opposite anchoring nail. Allow enough cord to tie two double half hitches to each spring and cut to this length.

2. Bring cord up to the top of the first coil spring and tie it with a double half hitch to the nearest rim of the first spring. Before drawing the knot tight, pull spring down to shape the seat or back. Continue to opposite side of the top on the same spring and tie it.

3. Continue in like fashion, tying two points on each spring and finally anchoring cord to nail on opposite side of frame. Run cords in both directions (side to side and front to back) at right angles to each other, until all springs are tied in two directions.

4. Tie springs diagonally in the same manner, beginning at one corner of the frame and anchoring cord on the opposite corner.

5. Repeat with cord at right angles to the first set of diagonal cords. Tie this cord to spring with two double half hitches and also tie it to the other three cords at their junction in the center of the coil. Each spring is now tied in eight places and the crossing cords are also tied together.

6. Replace padding.

Furring Strips

Pieces of wood attached to a surface so that another surface can be fastened to them are called furring strips. Normally, 1x2's are used for furring although ¼"x1" trim up to 1x4's can be used, depending upon the type and size of the work.

Furring strips are used when attaching vertical tongue-and-groove boards over studs and also are frequently necessary when attaching panel materials — hardboard, plywood, melamine plastic or cork laminated to hardboard, etc.—over existing walls. They are also used when putting up ceiling tiles.

Also see *ATTICS, BASEMENTS* and *WALLS.*

Furring strips, 1x2's, are nailed to the joists overhead and run at right angles to them. The ceiling tiles are then attached to the furring strips.

Furring is attached directly to the concrete block foundation wall to provide a nailing surface for these wood panels.

Photograph courtesy of Wood Conversion Company.

Fuses

Fuses are safety devices designed to protect the electrical lines and appliances within your home. They contain a special metal which melts when too much current is drawn through the electrical lines or if a short circuit occurs.

There are several different types of fuses used in the average household. They all do the same job—protect the electrical line—but are designed to fit different types of holders.

1. Cartridge fuses are generally used for heavy-duty work. They are normally used to protect the main service conductors leading into the home.

2. Glass fuses come in varying sizes, rated in amperes. Once the metal within them melts, the fuse must be replaced.

3. Thermal fuses are similar in appearance to the glass fuses but they are designed to carry a heavy starting load. For example, a 10-ampere thermal fuse will permit a momentary surge of current up to 20 amperes without breaking the circuit. If the current then drops to 10 amperes or less, the fuse will remain in operation. On the other hand, if the current remains above 10 amperes, the fuse will 'blow.' This type of fuse is frequently used on electrical lines with motors; they are desirable with stoker or oil burner motors or power tools in a workshop.

4. Miniature glass fuses are used to control low-current loads. They are generally used in cars but are also found in TV sets, tape and wire recorders and special light control units.

Here are four types of fuses with which the handyman comes into contact. On the left are two cartridge fuses; in the center are miniature glass fuses normally used for low electrical currents. Upper right is a standard glass fuse generally used to control branch circuit in the home. Lower right is a thermal fuse which will continue to function despite a momentary surge of current; this type of fuse is often used on electrical lines in workshops as well as furnace motors.

Gable

A gable roof.

This is an architectural term referring to the triangular end of an exterior wall above the eaves. It is also used to designate the shape of the room formed by a gable exterior wall.

Gage of Screw

The gage of a screw is its shank or diameter measured directly below the head.

When you purchase screws, you specify them according to *gage*, type of head, length and finish, where special finish is required. In the ac-companying table, you will find the screw designation by gage, the diameter in inches and the nearest fractional equivalent.

Gage of Screw		
Gage or Size	Basic Diameter	Fractional Equivalent (in inches)
0	.060	$1/16$
1	.073	$5/64$
2	.086	$3/32$
3	.099	$7/64$
4	.112	$7/64$
5	.125	$1/8$
6	.138	$9/64$
7	.151	$5/32$
8	.164	$11/64$
9	.177	$3/16$
10	.190	$3/16$
12	.216	$7/32$
14	.242	$1/4$
16	.286	$17/64$
18	.294	$19/64$
20	.320	$21/64$
24	.372	$3/8$

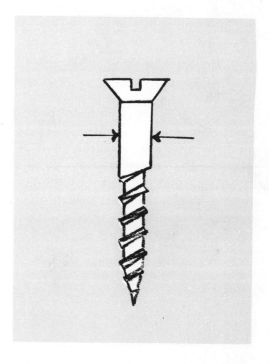

Gages and Indicators

Gages are measuring devices. They are special tools used because they are more convenient to handle or easier to read than the conventional rule or any of the regular rulers or micrometers.

The handyman has little need for any of the special gages unless he goes in for machine shop or lathe work in metal. There are four gages, however, which are more commonly used. They are:

1. the marking gage—used to mark off a set distance on the face or an edge of a board. See *Marking Gage*.

2. the drill bit gage—used to measure off a predetermined depth for drilling with a drill bit or auger. See *DEPTH GAGE*.

3. a feeler gage—generally used to check the points of the spark plug of your car.

4. a drill and screw gage—used to determine the size of a screw or drill bit.

There are many other special gages. Some are standard and are used frequently in machine shop or woodworking shop projects. Others are special and used only by the advanced craftsman and the professional.

A spark plug gap or feeler gage is used to check the space between the points of a plug.

Photograph courtesy of Anderson Associates, Inc.

A marking gage is used to mark off a preset distance along the face or on the edge of a board.

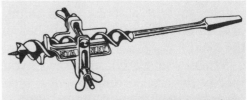

A drill bit gage is used to stop the boring of a hole beyond a specified depth.

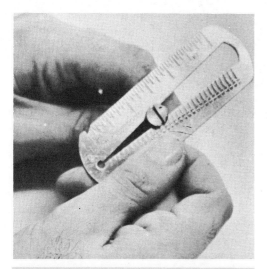

Screw gage is used to check the thickness or gage of the screw. Set screw into slot and read gage on scale at right where slot in screw matches scale line.

Contour gage is very useful in duplicating odd-shaped moldings. The thin slots of the gage can be adjusted to form the exact shape of any molding.

Feeler Gage

The feeler gage sometimes resembles a pocket knife with a lot of blades. All the blades have the same shape, but each blade is accurately ground to a definite thickness, which is stamped on the blade.

The feeler gage blades usually range in thickness from .0015" (about one-half the thickness of a hair on your head) to .025" (about the thickness of your thumb nail).

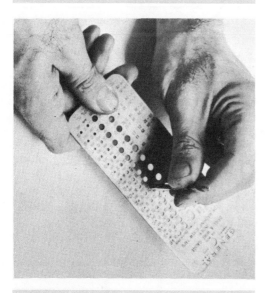

Drill and wire gage is used to verify exact size of drill bit. This is handy when the size of bit has been worn away or the drill bit is unmarked.

Here's a special type of gage which is used with a trimming knife to cut wallboard.

Photograph courtesy of Wallboard Tool Co.

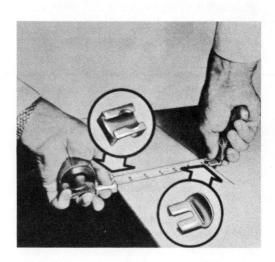

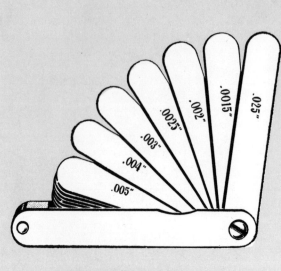

A FEELER GAGE

By selecting combinations of two or more blades you can measure any "gap" or clearance up to the total thickness of all the blades.

The thinner blades are placed between the heavier blades to prevent kinks and creases. When you use the thinner blades in combination, always try to protect them with the heavier blades of the combination. Wipe the blades with a clean cloth before you use them—otherwise your gage will not measure accurately. Films of oil, grease and dirt make a difference.

The secret of checking "gaps" and clearances accurately is your ability to "feel" the tension on the blade when you move it back and forth in the space you're measuring. The best way to develop this sense of feel is to practice measuring clearances of known dimensions.

Angle and Radius Gages

Angle gages and radius gages also have blades, but with them it's the blade outline that's important. Angle

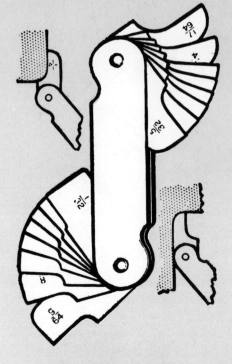

RADIUS GAGE

ANGLE GAGE

gage blades have the same thickness, but each blade has a different end angle. They are substitutes for the bevel protractor, and are indispensable for measuring angles in restricted areas where you couldn't possibly use the protractor.

A radius gage also has two sets of blades. The rounded corner of each blade is the arc of a circle. The radius of that arc is stamped on the blade. Examine one of these blades and you'll see that it can be used to check outside radii as well as inside radii.

Wire and Sheet Gages

The wire gage is used to measure cross-sections of wire and to determine the gage (thickness) of metal sheets. You could make these measurements with a micrometer or vernier caliper, but the simple circular gage is less expensive and a lot handier.

There are several kinds of sheet and wire gages, such as the United States Standard, the Imperial, and Birmingham gages. Before you use one of these gages be sure to remove the burrs from the sheet metal or wire that you are measuring.

Ring and Plug Gages

Ring gages are used to check the diameters of round machined parts such as shafts, rods and pins. They are carefully machined and ground to size, and each one has its size stamped on it.

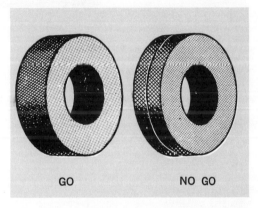

GO   NO GO

Ring gages are usually used in pairs of one "Go" gage and one "No Go" gage. If the size of the part being checked is within the specified dimensions, the "Go" gage will fit over the work. If the "No Go" gage can be fitted over the work, it's undersize.

Plug gages are used to check the diameters of holes. One common type is a combination "Go—No Go" gage. One end is ground to the minimum diameter allowed for the hole, and the other end is the maximum allowed diameter. Try to insert the ends of this gage into the hole you are measuring. The "Go" end should enter the hole. If the "No Go" end enters, the hole is too big. The diameter of a plug gage is stamped near the measuring surface.

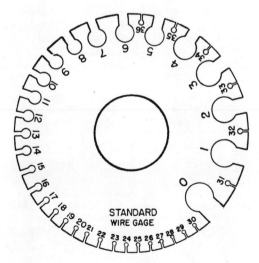

STANDARD WIRE GAGE

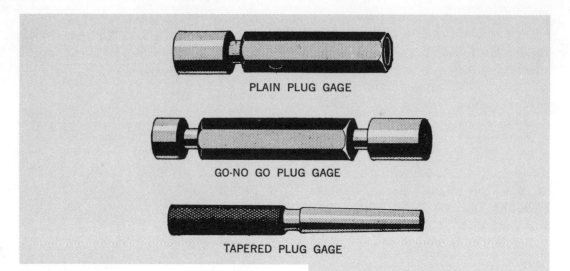

PLAIN PLUG GAGE

GO-NO GO PLUG GAGE

TAPERED PLUG GAGE

A tapered plug gage has a long round taper. Diameters may be marked at intervals. You can use one of these gages to estimate how much a hole is undersize or oversize. Special taper gages are used to check tapered holes.

Snap Gage

A snap gage is used in much the same way as a ring gage, but it can be used to check the outside diameters of shafts on which it is impossible (because of construction) to use a ring gage.

Adjustable snap gages have anvils that can be set to the desired dimensions with a micrometer or with gage blocks. The adjustable anvils are set, one for the allowable minimum diameter and the other for the allowable maximum diameter.

Gage Blocks

You may or may not get a chance to see—or use—a set of gage blocks, but you should know about them. These blocks are the ultimate in accuracy. They are used as master gages—other gages are set to them and checked against them.

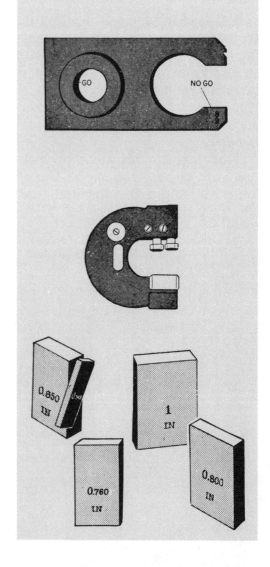

Gage blocks are manufactured in standard thicknesses. Combinations of two or more blocks are used to obtain any desired thickness. The best gage blocks are machined, ground and lapped so carefully that they are accurate within a few millionths of an inch. They are so close to being perfectly flat that two of the blocks will stick together when one is placed in contact with the other.

These gage blocks are often called "Jo-blocks" because the first really good ones were made by a man named Johansson. A complete set of Johansson gages includes 81 blocks.

Surface Gage

A surface gage is used to measure height, and for scribing layout lines on vertical surfaces. The commonly used universal type has a base plate, an adjustable extension arm, and an adjustable scriber. When a surface gage is set to a combination-square blade, both the square and the gage base must rest on a flat, smooth surface—preferably a surface plate.

You may have occasion to mount a dial indicator on the surface gage extension arm and use that set-up to check the trueness of round objects. A shaft may be checked in this way. You set the gage in position and turn the shaft slowly. If the shaft is not true the dial hand will indicate the deviation.

A dial indicator has a contact point that bears against a shaft or rod to check its alignment. The common dial indicator has a dial that's graduated in thousandths of an inch—both plus and minus.

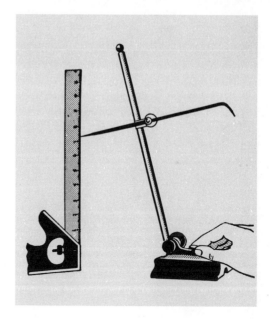

This indicator is often used to check the alignment of shafts. The base has T-slots, one of which is used to clamp the main post. This post has an adjustable clamp which holds the indicator arm in the desired position. The base should be clamped securely to a solid object when the dial indicator is being used.

Speed Indicator

When you need to know the number of revolutions per minute (RPM) of an electric motor, a line shaft, or other revolving part, you can easily secure the information with a speed indicator. It's also known as a revolution counter.

This tool has a set of interchangeable rubber tips that fit on the spindle. Cone-shaped, flat end, and vacuum tips are usually supplied with the indicator. The cup-like vacuum tip works best on the flat end of a shaft; the cone tip is best if the shaft has a countersunk end.

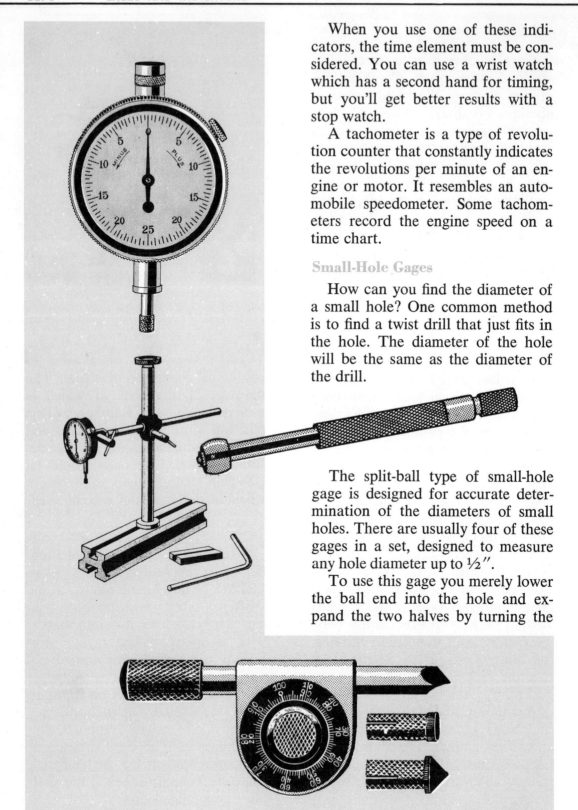

When you use one of these indicators, the time element must be considered. You can use a wrist watch which has a second hand for timing, but you'll get better results with a stop watch.

A tachometer is a type of revolution counter that constantly indicates the revolutions per minute of an engine or motor. It resembles an automobile speedometer. Some tachometers record the engine speed on a time chart.

Small-Hole Gages

How can you find the diameter of a small hole? One common method is to find a twist drill that just fits in the hole. The diameter of the hole will be the same as the diameter of the drill.

The split-ball type of small-hole gage is designed for accurate determination of the diameters of small holes. There are usually four of these gages in a set, designed to measure any hole diameter up to ½″.

To use this gage you merely lower the ball end into the hole and expand the two halves by turning the handle. When the "setting" is just right, lock the gage with the knob at the end of the handle. Then you can withdraw the gage from the hole and measure the "setting" with a micrometer or vernier.

Care of Gages and Indicators

All precision tools and instruments must be handled with the greatest care, and should be cased in special boxes or containers when they are not in use.

Precision tools won't retain their accuracy if allowed to become rusty, bent, or dented. That's why you must keep precision equipment coated with a thin film of clean oil to prevent rust, and adequately cased to prevent damage.

Never use emery cloth, sandpaper, steel wool, or any other abrasive to clean the moving parts of a precision tool or instrument. Those moving parts are machined and ground to exceptionally close tolerances. If you wear away some of the metal you ruin the fit of the parts and impair the accuracy.

Gain

The notch cut out, or technically, the shallow mortise or recess made in the frame of a doorway or the door itself to receive the hinge. It also refers to the cut-out in a timber to receive the end of a beam and to a groove made with the grain similar to a dado, which is made across the grain.

Galvanized Iron

Iron is galvanized by undergoing a cleaning process and then being dipped into a bath of molten zinc. This forms a protective coat to retard oxidation or rusting. However, exposure to the elements wears the zinc coating away and then the iron rusts, unless the surface is protected. Galvanized iron was widely used, and is still used to a lesser extent, for downspouts and gutters.

Proper care of galvanized metal involves brushing the surface clean and applying a finish coat. There are special zinc coating paints available or you can use any good exterior grade paint, which will adhere better if the galvanized metal has weathered for about six months. Where the galvanized iron is not visible, for example the inner section of a gutter, asphalt can be applied to prolong the metal's life.

Gambrel Roof

This is a roof which has its slope broken by an obtuse angle.

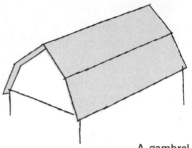

A gambrel roof.

Garage

If you need a shelter for the family car and if you'd like to have some extra space for storage or a small workshop, you should plan on adding a garage to your home. Garages, to be functional, should be well planned. Even if you do not build it yourself, you should read through the following pages to get ideas on how to plan a driveway, the type of door best suited for your needs,

and how to dress up your garage with unusual doors.

Planning a Garage

First of all, of course, garages must meet the primary need of providing protection for the family car or cars. But if you plan adequately before you build the garage, you can also provide added space for storage, and avoid overflowing closets or an overcrowded basement in the home itself. Or you can provide for any number of uses that add to the everyday enjoyment of living.

And here's something important to remember: it costs about half as much to provide extra space in the garage as it does to add an equal amount of space in building a home.

SHELTER FOR YOUR CAR

A garage represents a modest but very wise investment in shelter, because it protects a relatively large investment in your car.

Thus your garage protects your car from the weather, from rain, snow, sleet, ice, dust, dirt, sun, which damage chassis and car body. It safeguards the car from petty thievery of parts, such as hub caps, and from theft of the car itself. It insures the car against damage by mischievous children and pranksters.

A garage raises the value of residential property. If well designed, it adds attractiveness as well as utility. It increases the selling price if and when you wish to sell.

Sketch courtesy of Strand Garage Door Division, Detroit Steel Corp.

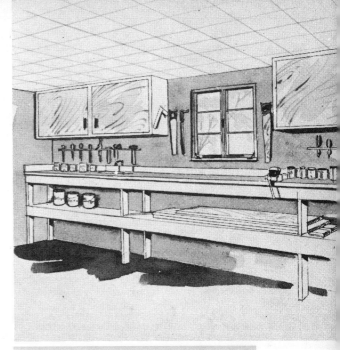

The extra space in a 1½ car garage can be used for a full-sized workbench for repairs and the pursuit of a favorite hobby.

NEED STORAGE SPACE?

It's no special secret that for a great many years, homes have been "shrinking" in size. With today's construction costs, you don't find many new homes with the generously pro-

A porch at the side of a garage provides a spot for the entire family to enjoy their leisure hours, during the warm weather.

portioned rooms and the spacious clothes closets and attic space found in the homes built several decades ago. Perhaps that's why one of the most popular uses for extra room in the garage is to provide needed storage space.

Properly designed, the garage can be used to store garden tools of all kinds, screens, storm windows, storm doors, ladders, sleds, bicycles. Or it might provide storage space instead for the lawn and porch furniture, swings, seats, boats, fertilizer, paint and paint brushes and other useful articles.

ADD TO LIVING SPACE

If there are times when it would be a relief to have the youngsters off somewhere by themselves, you can provide space in your garage for a children's playroom. Or you can build on a porch where all members of the family can relax in nice weather; and you can screen it for summer comfort.

Many people use a section of the garage for enjoyment of a hobby (after all, a workbench doesn't take up much space!). Such hobbies cover a very large range, but in each case they provide welcome relaxation and add a new interest to life. The number of alternate uses for a garage is almost unlimited, such as providing a place for a flower sink, lavatory (in a heated garage), wardrobe closet for sporting and rain togs, a cabinet opening outdoors for garden equipment, a doghouse, or an incinerator.

The use of a little imagination and ingenuity can make your garage an important feature of the home.

TYPE OF ARCHITECTURE

The type of architecture you choose for your garage should, usually, be the same as the architecture of your home. If your home is not a definite type of architecture, then choose a garage that suits your own taste.

The type of roof you select for your garage should, of course, harmonize with the architecture of your home. In most instances, a roof of the same type as the roof of your home will assure you of the proper harmony. Usually, you get an effect pleasing to the eye by having the roof of the garage parallel to the roof of the house, or nearly so.

It is usually best, wherever possible, to use the same material in the construction of your garage as you have used in building your home. This is not an absolute rule, however, as a brick colonial house with white trim can very well be complemented by a white frame garage.

The Garage Door

It is best to make the garage door as wide as possible, at least 9′, to allow for free movement of a new car. The wider door gives you the added clearance you need and makes

Solid masonry with jambs.

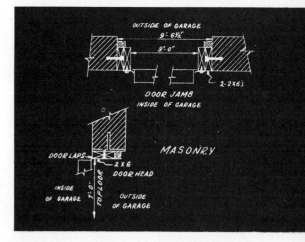

Sketches courtesy of Strand Garage Door Division, Detroit Steel Corp.

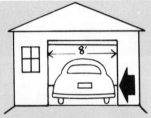

Wide new cars make it a tight squeeze getting into the conventional 8' garage opening. And it's worse if you have to make a turn to get inside.

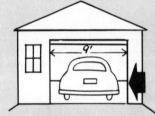

However, a 9' wide garage door saves on fender repair bills and makes it easy to get the car in and out of the garage.

your garage better for both housing and servicing your car. Furthermore, it permits you to move things in and out without danger of scratching your car. The wider door is a "must" if you have a baby carriage or a child's bike stored inside the garage with a car.

How To Frame A
Garage Doorway

Proper preparation of the garage door opening is important if doors are to be installed quickly, easily and are to operate satisfactorily! Hardware of the type illustrated is jamb-hung—both for canopy and receding doors.

There are only four important

Wood frame.

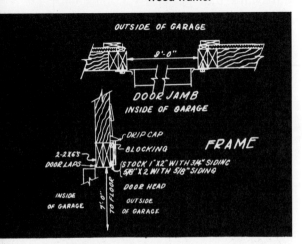

points to watch:

1. Use lumber for side jambs that is of good quality, straight, strong and securely fastened to the construction. This member must be a minimum of 1⅝" thick (2 x 4 or 2 x 6). Do not use 1" lumber for casing.

2. Be sure that inside face of header trim (usually 1" lumber) is flush with inside face of side jamb.

3. Opening dimension in both width and height must be maintained uniformly for the entire opening. Expense and trouble will be avoided if this is watched carefully. For example:

The 8'0", 9'0" or 16'0" width dimensions must be the same at the top, middle and bottom of the opening. The same applies for the height dimension of 7'0". This must be the same at both sides and the middle.

4. Openings must be square and plumb. (You can easily check for plumbness by running a string diagonally from top to bottom corners. If the strings touch at the point in the center where they pass each other, the opening is plumb.) Watch the floor construction if the level of the garage floor is to be higher than the drive. A slope from the inside face of side jamb to the outside is recommended.

Garage—Doors

Carved panel doors add richness to the exterior of this home.

There are many types of doors you can use with your garage. If you are building a garage or modernizing an old one, you will find the overhead type more convenient.

You can make garage doors behave! Gone are the days of struggle with sliding doors or banging your fenders on swinging doors that stubbornly refused either to stay open or remain closed.

By putting in a day's work, you can equip your garage with a convenient modern door that swings up overhead out of the way almost at the touch of a finger.

Here are the ways to keep down the cost of such a door:

• Buy hardware and lumber and build a new door, using one of several practical designs for the job.

• Buy the hardware and convert an existing pair of swinging doors to a single overhead door.

• Buy an overhead-door kit, assemble the door and install it with hardware that generally comes with the kit.

Any of these three procedures should save you money compared with ordering a ready-made door, either of wood or metal, and paying a carpenter to put it up. However, there are some doors that are unusually attractive and you may not be skilled enough to make ornamental wood doors, or you might prefer to get a ready-made metal door and install it yourself. No matter which you choose, you will be satisfied with

Here's another example of carved wood panel garage doors.

Photographs courtesy of Raynor Manufacturing Co.

the marked improvement in the appearance of your garage.

Types of Hardware

Three basic types of hardware are used to mount overhead doors and swing them up and down—jamb, pivot and track.

Jamb hardware is attached to the inside edges of the two upright wood members (the jambs) that form the sides of the garage door opening. It works by leverage.

Pivot hardware is bolted to the side walls of the garage and works the door by swinging it up and down. This type is not easily installed when the garage itself is much wider than the opening.

Jamb and pivot hardware is suitable only for one-piece, rigid doors that tilt or swing up and down. With the track type, you can have either a rigid swing-up door or a sectional roll-up kind. Roller-bearing wheels moving on steel tracks make such doors easiest to operate. Unlike doors mounted with jamb or pivot hardware, these doors can be weather-stripped. Hence, track doors are most popular in cold regions. However, they cost more.

Hardware should be selected to suit the weight of the door. Most sets are safe only if the door weighs less than 150 pounds. If your door exceeds that figure, you should buy heavy-duty hardware.

Track for Roll-Up Door

Jamb Type

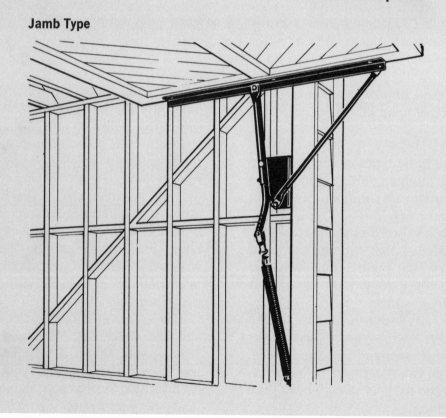

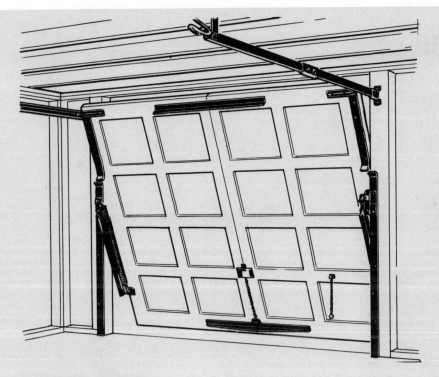

Track for Swing Door

Offset Pivot

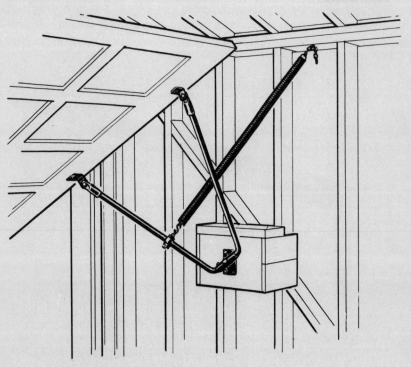

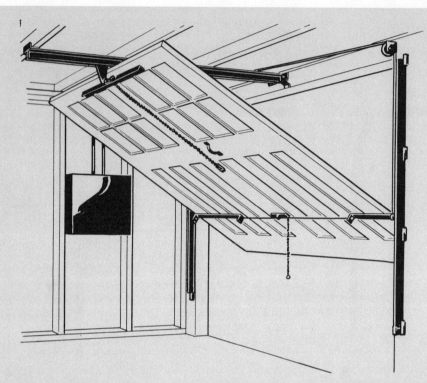

Track with Counterbalance

Swinging doors can be converted to the overhead type by screwing angle iron to the top and bottom edges to make them a single rigid unit.

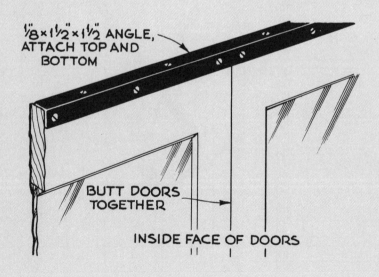

$\frac{1}{8}$" × 1$\frac{1}{2}$" × 1$\frac{1}{2}$ ANGLE, ATTACH TOP AND BOTTOM

BUTT DOORS TOGETHER

INSIDE FACE OF DOORS

Carved Wood Doors

If you want something different and attractive in the way of garage doors, you might consider carved panel doors. While the advanced handyman can make doors of this type, the average homeowner is less skilled. There are many types of carved wood doors from which to choose.

Making Your Own Doors

Here are several ideas for you if you like to make your own unusual garage doors. They are prize-winning selections from a contest for designers run by Arts & Architecture and the Tavart Co., manufacturers of overhead-door hardware. Pick your own prize-winner and get to work in your shop.

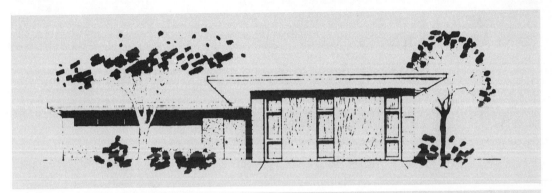

Broken surface of this door creates interesting lights and shadows. By varying the surface panels, you can match the forms of the house so that the door will be a well-integrated unit. Vary the levels of the two horizontal pieces to match the nearest window sill and transom. Set and putty the nails or screws to hold the facing frame.

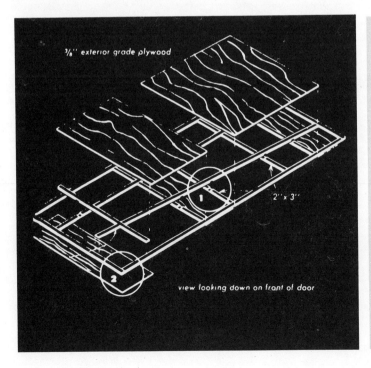

⅜" exterior grade plywood

2" x 3"

view looking down on front of door

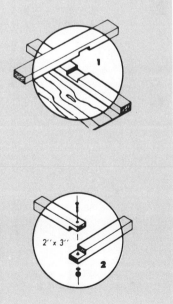

2" x 3"

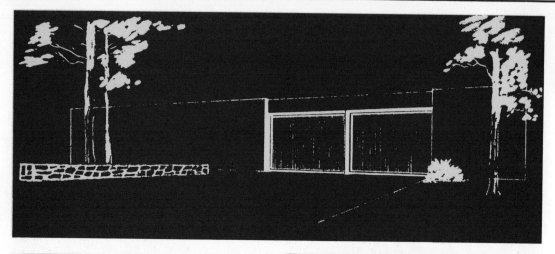

Translucent corrugated panels of reinforced fiber glass are used as the closure material for this handsome door. Assemble the rear frame from 2x4's and use 2x2's to hold the panels.

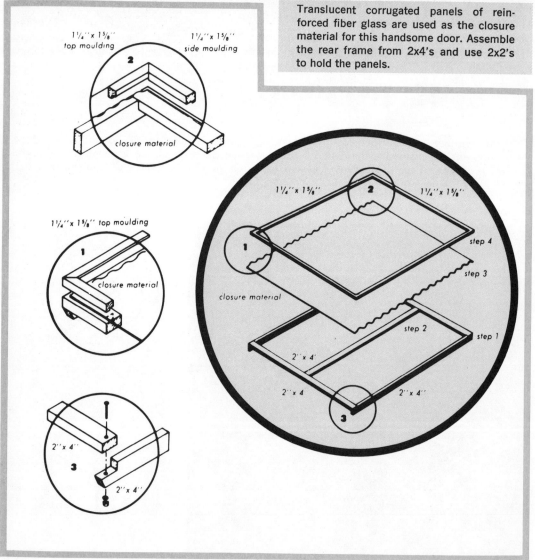

For this basket-weave door, you need five pieces of 2x6, 7' long, and strips of ¼" Masonite. Glue and screw the tempered Masonite to the wood stiles, keeping butt joints on the rear of the door.

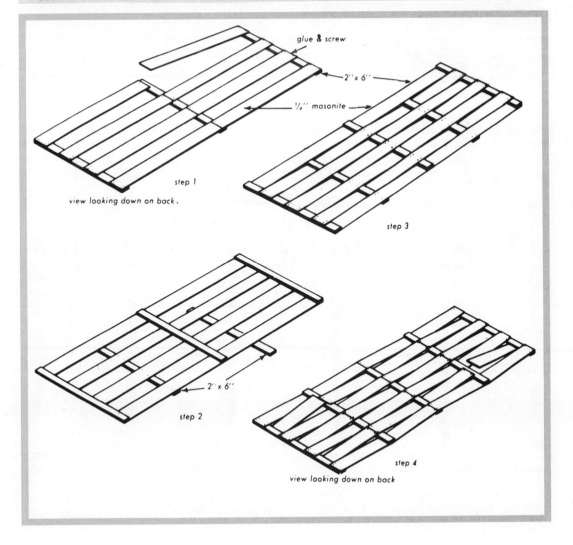

Framing creates the design here. One or more of the plywood panels can be replaced with translucent sheet material. Plywood can be left natural or painted, depending upon the effect you wish to create.

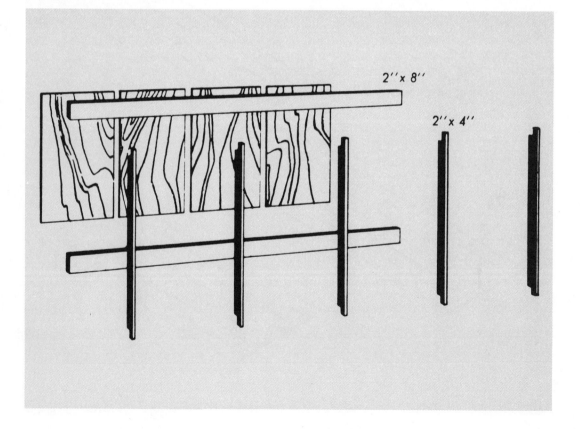

2'' x 8''

2'' x 4''

Garage— Driveway

The driveway is very important. Whether is it long or short, the driveway should be practical, and planned to meet your needs. It is well to allow as much room as possible for both turning and clearance rather than figuring too closely. Be sure to build a driveway that will serve you without daily inconvenience or possible damage to your car.

In planning your driveway there are several important things to consider, in addition to your decision as to type, length, etc. The dimensions of the car, or cars, which will be using the driveway must be taken into consideration. When planning the spaces provided for parking and turning it is well to measure the over-all length (not wheelbase) of these cars. The smallest automobiles measure 11′ 7½″ in length, the average 18′ 0″, and the largest 19′ 7″. It is evident, from these figures, that there can be a great deal of variance in the dimensions of driveways constructed for different cars. The width of your car, or cars, should also be taken into consideration.

The width of the smallest car is 4′ 1″, the average 6′ 6″, and the largest 6′ 10″. In planning your driveway, it is suggested that a clear-

Typical Driveway Sections

1. The ribbon drive is an economical concrete drive, but not very satisfactory when curves are required.
2. The solid drive is best for driving ease and maintenance.
3. The gravel drive is most economical to install and thus is ideally suited for the long driveways in suburban areas.

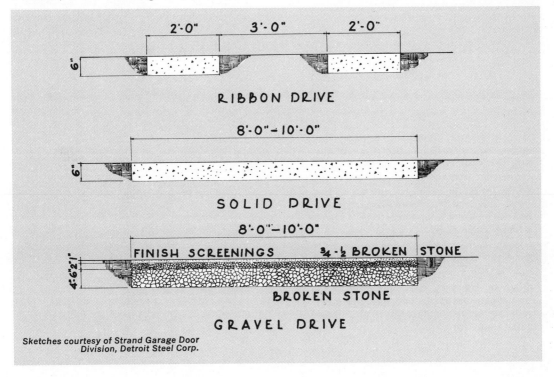

RIBBON DRIVE

SOLID DRIVE

GRAVEL DRIVE

Sketches courtesy of Strand Garage Door Division, Detroit Steel Corp.

ance of 1' 6" be allowed from the edge of the drive to any objects, shrubs, etc.

If your present car is narrower than some of today's car models, you should also take into account the fact that the next car you own may need greater driveway width for trouble-free operation of the car.

When a car makes a turn, the rear wheels do not follow in the tracks of the front wheels. The drive, therefore, must be wider on the turns than on the straight sections. It is suggested that on gradual turns a minimum of 10' 0" be used. For greater than average turning radius, or greater turning speeds, a wider drive is de-

sirable. The ease of driving depends largely upon the uniformity of curvature of the drive. The speed permissible is dependent upon the width of the drive.

Also see *DRIVEWAYS* and *CONCRETE*.

Three Popular Driveway Layouts

If you have the room, it is better to lay out a large driveway. Not only will you have more room to maneuver, but you'll have that extra space for parking for guests.

Here are three popular driveway layouts from which to choose. Other types of layouts are included in the section *DRIVEWAYS*.

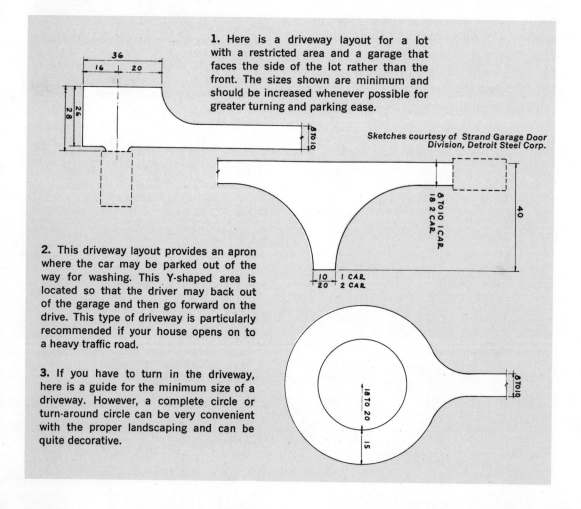

1. Here is a driveway layout for a lot with a restricted area and a garage that faces the side of the lot rather than the front. The sizes shown are minimum and should be increased whenever possible for greater turning and parking ease.

Sketches courtesy of Strand Garage Door Division, Detroit Steel Corp.

2. This driveway layout provides an apron where the car may be parked out of the way for washing. This Y-shaped area is located so that the driver may back out of the garage and then go forward on the drive. This type of driveway is particularly recommended if your house opens on to a heavy traffic road.

3. If you have to turn in the driveway, here is a guide for the minimum size of a driveway. However, a complete circle or turn-around circle can be very convenient with the proper landscaping and can be quite decorative.

Garage—Plans

Photographs courtesy of Insulite Division, Minnesota and Ontario Paper Co.

In this section, you will find step-by-step information on how to build a frame garage. The preliminary work is the same if you wish to use masonry. See the sections on *CONCRETE, CONCRETE BLOCKS* and *FOUNDATION* for how-to details.

Frame Garage

The first plan is for a gable roof garage. You can, however, with a few modifications, turn the garage into a double garage, a single-car garage with shed roof, or a single garage with a built-in porch or breezeway. See sections on *Porch* and *Roofs*.

1. PREPARING THE SITE— The first step in the job should be the preparation of the site for the concrete slab. The site should be

1. Mark off the site with string. Level it and dig footings to a depth below the frost line. This foundation was constructed of 8″ concrete blocks and waterproofed.

level, and the ground should be packed down. Mark out the site with stakes and string, leaving an extra two feet for a concrete apron, if desired. Then put in form boards— 2x8's will do a good job for a 4″ or 6″ slab. Drive stakes on the outside of the form boards. Several inches of sand or gravel fill should be spread over the site (to allow proper seepage of the water from the concrete) and should be well tamped.

2. POURING THE CONCRETE SLAB—A 4″ slab was poured for the model garage. Readymixed concrete was used, making for a much faster and easier operation. A rake and a shovel are the only tools needed to spread the concrete evenly inside the forms. Jab the shovel blade into the

2. A 4″ slab—reinforced with No. 9 mesh —was poured with ready-mixed concrete.

wet concrete to make sure all air pockets are removed. Then, with a friend or neighbor on one end of a long 2x4, and yourself at the other end, work the 2x4 back and forth in a saw-like motion ("screeding") across the entire surface of the slab, After the surface is troweled and the

apron is tapered, set in anchor bolts according to the directions on your plan or blueprint. Finally, cover the slab with burlap or similar cloth, and keep damp for several days until it is properly "cured." See *Concrete.*

FRAMING THE WALLS— You'll save considerable time and effort if you put the framing together for each wall (with 16d nails) while it is lying flat on the ground,

3. To frame the walls, drill holes through the nailing sill for the slab anchor bolts. Place studs 16″ o.c.

4. Determine the pitch of the garage roof. Front and rear rafters go on first. Toenail rafters to ridge board with 8d nails. Put up a pair of rafters at a time, checking the ridge board occasionally. Pre-cut the notches and rafter ends to save time.

5. Sheathe the walls next. Big 4'x8' boards can be used for the sidewalls and 2'x8' boards for the gable ends. Run the sheathing up and around rafter ends to give a perfectly tight, well-insulated wall.

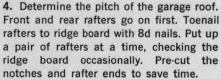

Photographs courtesy of Insulite Division, Minnesota and Ontario Paper Co.

6. Sheathe the roof with standard 1x8 lumber. The roof boards are nailed to the rafters with 8d nails, two nails per board per rafter. Stagger the butt ends so joints fall on different rafters.

7. If asphalt shingles are used, apply a layer of 15# felt on the roof, then a double layer of shingles as the bottom row on each side. Project the shingles ½" at the eaves and ¼" at gables for drip edge.

before raising it into vertical position at the edge of the slab. The model garage was framed with studs on 16″ centers. Drill holes through the sole plate for the slab anchor bolts. Then raise the framed wall section into vertical position. Insert anchor bolts through the holes in the sole plate, and screw on nuts. Then go ahead and frame the next section in the same manner. After all the wall sections are bolted to the slab, run joists between the sidewalls to serve as ties, and toenail these to the top plate with 10d nails. A 2x4 joist every four feet will provide an adequate tie between the two opposite walls.

4. FRAMING THE ROOF— Now that the walls are framed, it's time to frame the roof. The angle of the roof pitch will determine the angle at which the rafter ends should be cut. The roof pitch, of course, will also determine the angle of the rafter-ends notches, which should be cut so they have 3″ bearing on the plate. Put up front and rear rafters first, using 2x4's. Toenail rafters to ridge board with 8d nails. Then nail other end to plate or joists using 16d nails. Put up a pair of the rafters at a time, checking the level of the ridge board occasionally as you go along. A board run from the ridge board to a joists will help maintain level.

5. ADDING ROOF SHEATHING—The next step is the sheathing of the roof—with standard 1x8 lumber. The roof boards are nailed to the rafters with 8d nails—two nails per board per rafter. Stagger the butt ends so that two joints aren't next to each other, vertically on the same rafter. Then cover the roof with 15-pound asphalt felt, before applying asphalt shingles.

6. ADDING WALL SHEATHING—In this particular model, 4-foot-wide boards of Insulite Bildrite Sheathing (an insulating sheathing made of asphalt-impregnated wood fibers) were used to sheath the walls. They are a vital part of a garage like this because they provide bracing strength twice that of wood sheathing. They also add efficient insulation, and protection against rain and moisture. The sheathing is marked where the nails should go —every 3″ on the outside edges and every 1″ on intermediate studs.

7. INSTALLING ROOF SHINGLES—Now you're ready to put the asphalt shingles on the roof. It is important to apply a double layer of shingles at the bottom row on each side of the roof, with the top edge of the bottom layer turned downward. Overlap the shingles ½″ at the eaves, ¼″ at the gables for a dip edge. Drive 1″ galvanized roofing nails ½″ above the slots on each shingle, and 1″ from each edge (total of four nails for each shingle).

Stagger the next course so that neither slots nor edges fall over the slots or edges of the lower course. A metal strip is applied over the ridge after the shingle application is completed. (See application instructions contained in shingle cartons.) The next step is to finish off the eaves, according to your plan or blueprint.

8. INSTALLING WALL SHINGLES—Insulite Shingle-Backer (a

8. Finish the exterior to harmonize with the exterior of the house. Here, clear cedar siding was used, and metal corner caps were used on the corners.

9. The overhead doors are installed before the final painting. Follow the manufacturer's directions which come with the hardware.

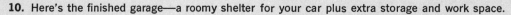

10. Here's the finished garage—a roomy shelter for your car plus extra storage and work space.

⁵⁄₁₆″-thick, wood-fibre insulation board) was selected as the undercourse material for the wood-shingled walls of the model garage because of the greater ease and speed of application compared to wood undercourse shingles, and because it provided more insulation and moisture-resistance.

9. ADDING THE OVERHEAD DOOR—To install the overhead type of door, follow the manufacturers' instructions closely.

Contemporary Garage Plans

Maybe you'd like to build a garage to go with a contemporary home and use contemporary materials. Rein-forced fiber glass plastic or polyester panels are durable, attractive and translucent.

For the more advanced handyman who wishes to build it himself or the homeowner who'd like to have a garage built for him, we have included a set of four different contemporary garage plans.

The Annex is an example of an attached garage which can be the answer for the family with storage problems. The back exit doors of the garage can be sliding doors, both opening to the left. Storage space goes back to the first translucent panel on the side. This shed roof garage combines plastic panels with plywood.

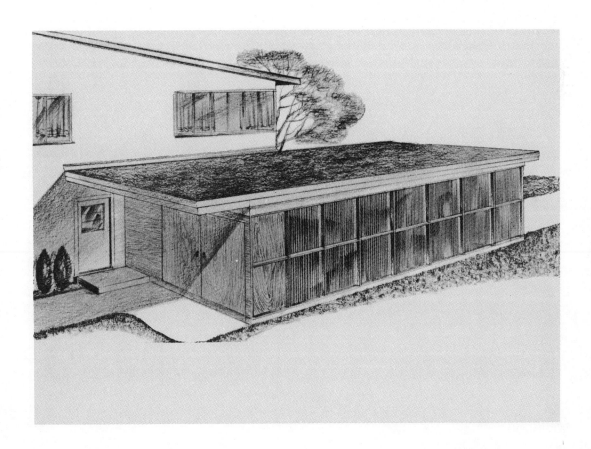

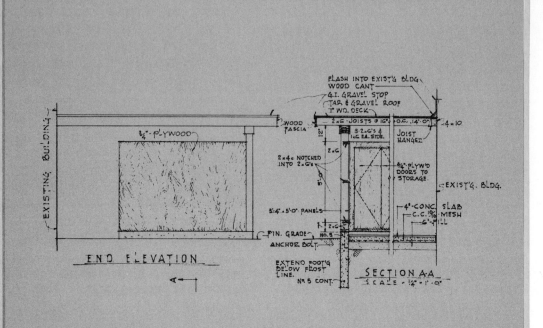

FLASH INTO EXIST'G BLDG
WOOD CANT
G.I. GRAVEL STOP
TAR & GRAVEL ROOF
1" WD. DECK

WOOD
FASCIA

3/4" PLYWOOD

2×6 JOISTS @ 16" O.C. 14'-0"
3-2.6'S &
1×6 EA. SIDE.

4×10

JOIST
HANGER

2×4= NOTCHED
INTO 2×6's

2×6

3/4" PLYW'D
DOORS TO
STORAGE

EXIST'G. BLDG.

3'-4"× 5'-0" PANELS

2×6

4" CONC. SLAB
C.C. 19/6 MESH
6"× FILL

FIN. GRADE
ANCHOR BOLT

NO.5

END ELEVATION

EXTEND FOOT'G
BELOW FROST
LINE.

Nº 5 CONT.

SECTION A-A
SCALE - 1/4" = 1'-0"

END ELEVATION

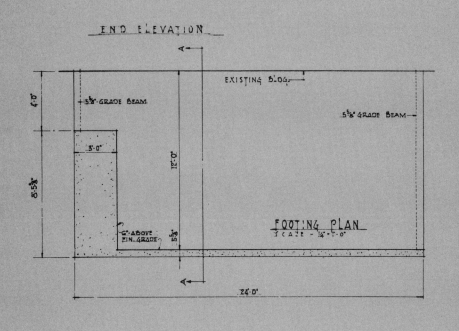

EXISTING BLDG.

4'-0"

5 3/8" GRADE BEAM

5 3/8" GRADE BEAM

3'-0"

12'-0"

8'-5 3/8"

5 3/8"

6" ABOVE
FIN. GRADE

FOOTING PLAN
SCALE - 1/4" = 1'-0"

24'-0"

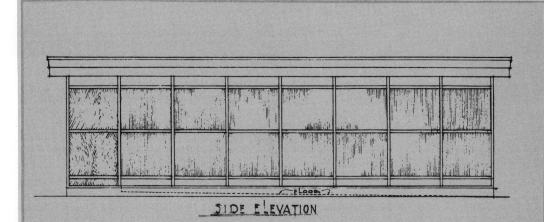

SIDE ELEVATION

Sketches courtesy of Monsanto Chemical Co.

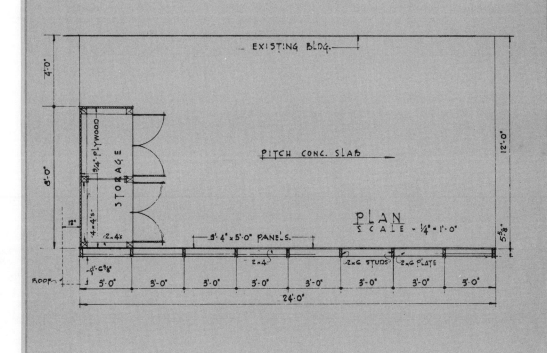

The Sky Lighter is a garage that lets you work inside in a blaze of glory. Not only does it have a full transparent or translucent roof, but there are five narrow panels along the side to permit light to fill the garage.

Sketches courtesy of Monsanto Chemical Co.

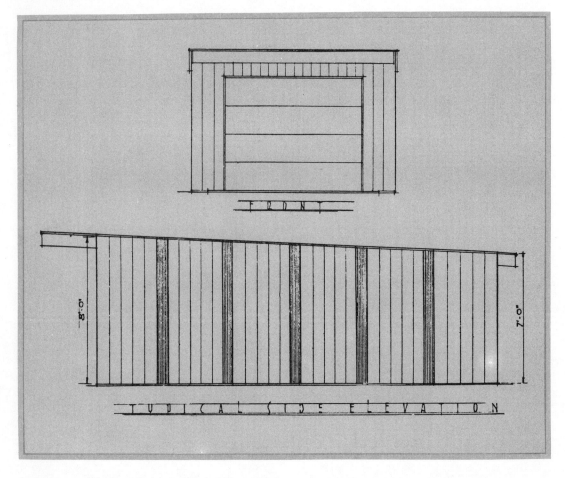

FRONT

8'-0"   7'-0"

TYPICAL SIDE ELEVATION

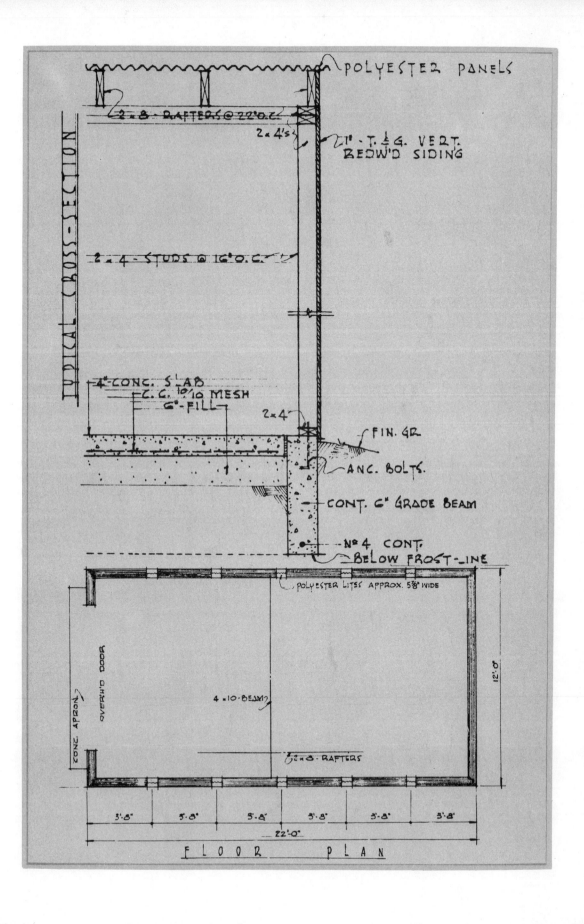

POLYESTER PANELS

TYPICAL CROSS-SECTION

2 × 8 RAFTERS @ 22" O.C.

2 × 4's

1" T.&G. VERT.
REDW'D SIDING

2 × 4 STUDS @ 16" O.C.

4" CONC. SLAB
Z.C. 10/10 MESH
6" FILL

2 × 4

FIN. GR.

ANC. BOLTS.

CONT. 6" GRADE BEAM

Nº 4 CONT.
BELOW FROST-LINE

POLYESTER LITES APPROX. 5⅝" WIDE

CONC. APRON

OVERH'D DOOR

4 × 10 BEAM?

12'-0"

2 × 8 RAFTERS

3'-8" | 3'-8" | 3'-8" | 3'-8" | 3'-8" | 3'-8"

22'-0"

FLOOR PLAN

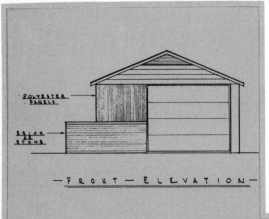

— F R O N T — E L E V A T I O N —

POLYESTER PANELS

BRICK OR STONE

The City Gardener is the solution for storing the car and garden equipment. This garage is a combination greenhouse and car shelter with a starting bench and planting box outside to take the transplants. The translucent roof and sidewalls give day-brightness to the garage and ample light for starting plants.

Sketches courtesy of Monsanto Chemical Co.

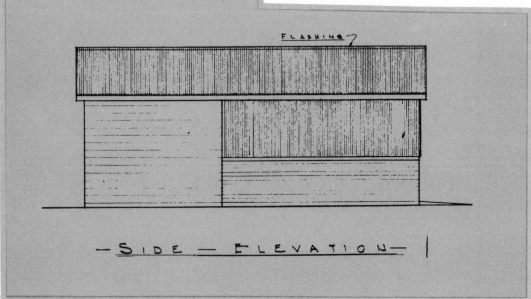

FLASHING

— S I D E — E L E V A T I O N —

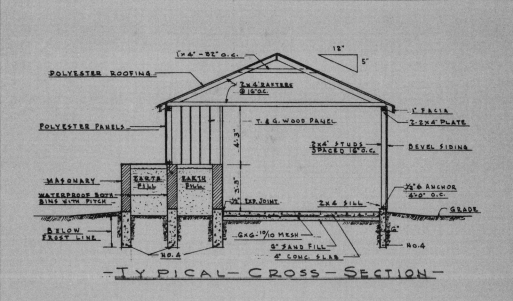

POLYESTER ROOFING

1"x 4" - 32" O.C.

2x4 RAFTERS @ 16" O.C.

12"
5"

1" FACIA

T. & G. WOOD PANEL

2-2x4" PLATE

POLYESTER PANELS

4'·3"

2x4" STUDS SPACED 16" O.C.

BEVEL SIDING

MASONARY

EARTH FILL

EARTH FILL

3'·3"

½"Ø ANCHOR 4'-0" O.C.

WATERPROOF BOTH BINS WITH PITCH

½" EXP. JOINT

2x4 SILL

GRADE

BELOW FROST LINE

NO.4

6x6·10/10 MESH

6" SAND FILL

4" CONC. SLAB

6"

No.4

—TYPICAL—CROSS—SECTION—

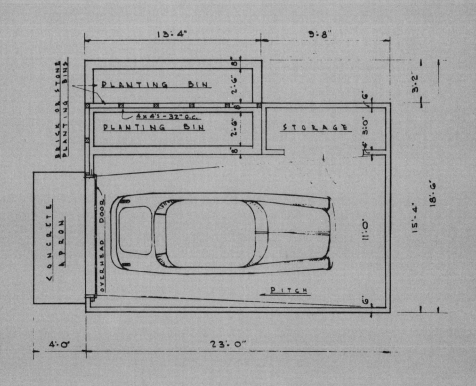

13'·4"   9'·8"

BRICK OR STONE PLANTING BINS

8"

PLANTING BIN

2'·6"

3'·2"

PLANTING BIN

4x4'S - 32" O.C.

2'·6"

8"

STORAGE

6"

3'·0"

6"

CONCRETE APRON

OVERHEAD DOOR

11'·0"

18'·6"

15'·4"

PITCH

6"

4'·0"   23'·0"

— FLOOR — PLAN —

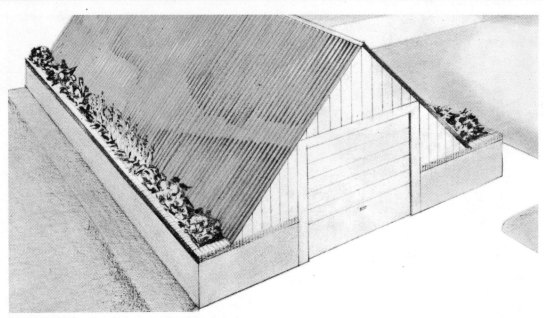

The Diamond Point is ideal for northern latitudes where there's lots of snow or for windy coasts where roof-ripping gales are common. The load-bearing roof beams brace each other and give ample over-the-car space to store a boat, screens, storm sash or many of the everyday items every homeowner needs to store. This unusual garage has short masonry walls over which large polyester panels are set.

Sketches courtesy of Monsanto Chemical Co.

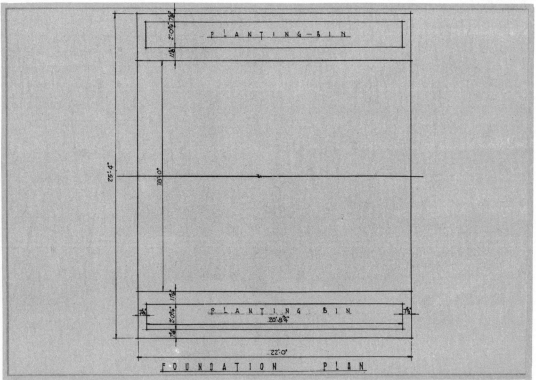

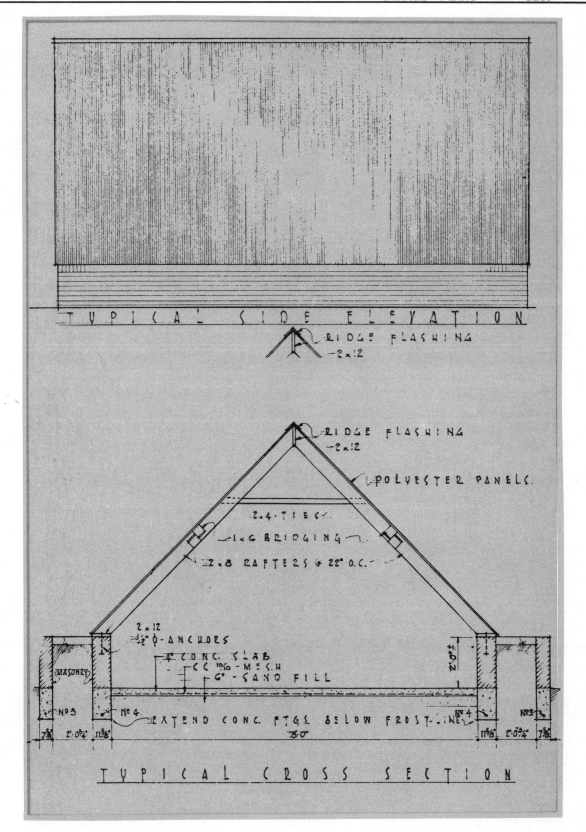

TYPICAL SIDE ELEVATION

RIDGE FLASHING
—2 x 12

RIDGE FLASHING
—2 x 12

POLYESTER PANELS

2-4 TIES

1 x 6 BRIDGING

2 x 8 RAFTERS @ 22" O.C.

2 x 12

½" Ø ANCHORS

4" CONC. SLAB

6 x 6 10/10 MESH

6" SAND FILL

MASONRY

2'-0"±

No 3   No 4   EXTEND CONC. FTGS BELOW FROST LINE   No 4   No 3

7½" 2'-0¾" 11⅜"   8'-0"   11⅜" 2'-0¾" 7½"

TYPICAL CROSS SECTION

Garage—Finishing the Interior

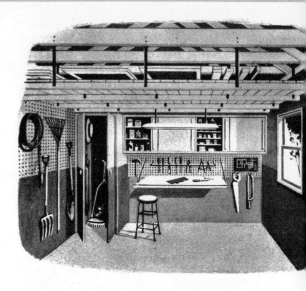

A neat and trim look can be given the inside walls of your garage by lining them with tempered hardboard from base to wainscot height and then placing perforated hardboard above. With interchangeable pegboard metal fixtures you can store any number of garden and lawn tools in the arrangement you want.

The average wood frame garage will have wall studs placed at intervals of 16″ on centers. Sufficient furring strips, joists or headers should be installed so that all edges of each panel will bear on a continuous support (see sketch A). If studs are farther than 16″ o.c., intermediate studs should be installed so that maximum distance between nailing bases is 16″.

Hardboard is readily cut with hand or power saws. Cut with smooth side up. A crosscut saw is

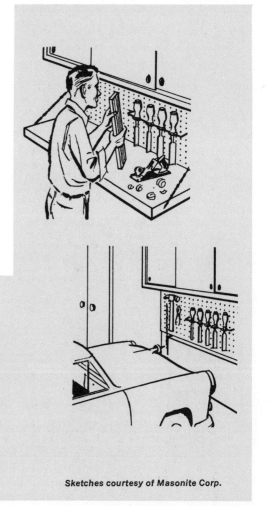

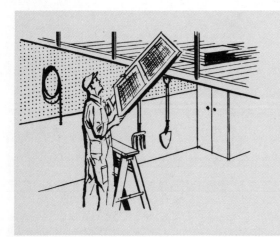

Sketches courtesy of Masonite Corp.

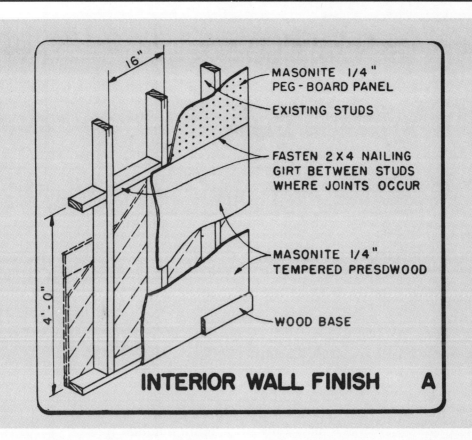

16"

MASONITE 1/4"
PEG-BOARD PANEL

EXISTING STUDS

FASTEN 2 X 4 NAILING
GIRT BETWEEN STUDS
WHERE JOINTS OCCUR

MASONITE 1/4"
TEMPERED PRESDWOOD

4'-0"

WOOD BASE

INTERIOR WALL FINISH   A

most suitable. Compass saw is used for cutting irregular edges.

Fit panels loosely so they will not have to be forced into place. Leave a slight space at the joints. Use 3d, 1¼", nails spaced 6" apart at intermediate supports and 4" apart around the edges. Nail center first, edges last. Do not nail closer than ¼" to any edge.

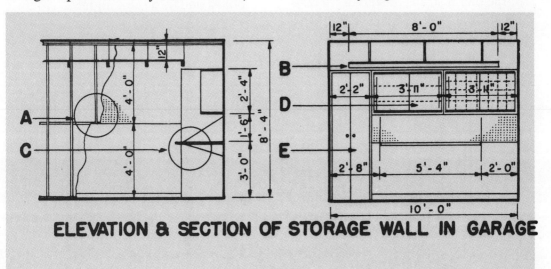

ELEVATION & SECTION OF STORAGE WALL IN GARAGE

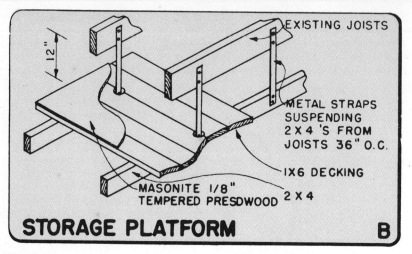

STORAGE PLATFORM   **B**

12″

EXISTING JOISTS

METAL STRAPS
SUSPENDING
2 X 4 'S FROM
JOISTS 36″ O.C.

IX6 DECKING

MASONITE 1/8″
TEMPERED PRESDWOOD   2 X 4

Storage Platform

For screens, storm windows, lumber, etc. (see sketch B), you can put a lot of waste space to work by suspending a convenient storage platform from the existing joists of your garage. With hardboard nailed onto the decking of the platform, you will have a smooth, flat surface that will not scratch or snag whatever you want to store.

Apply decking to 2x4's spaced the same distance apart as the joists. Then lay the ⅛″ hardboard on the deck and use 3d, 1¼″, nails spaced 12″ apart throughout the panel and 4″ apart around the edges. Drill holes for the metal straps, fasten to the 2x4 and then fasten the entire platform to the joists.

Worktable

Here is the center of your garage workshop (see sketch C). For a smooth, splinter-free work surface you can use ¾″ hardboard. When lowered against the wall, it will take only ¾″ from the total length of your garage, so you will still be able to get your car inside. This table can be built along the side of your garage just as well as the end—whichever is more suitable.

After wall panels are in place, studs can easily be located through the perforations in the pegboard panel. Be sure hinges of table are securely fastened through the hardboard and into the studding.

Sketches courtesy of Masonite Corp.

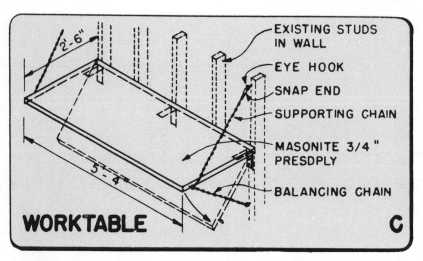

WORKTABLE   **C**

2′-6″

5′-4″

EXISTING STUDS
IN WALL

EYE HOOK

SNAP END

SUPPORTING CHAIN

MASONITE 3/4″
PRESDPLY

BALANCING CHAIN

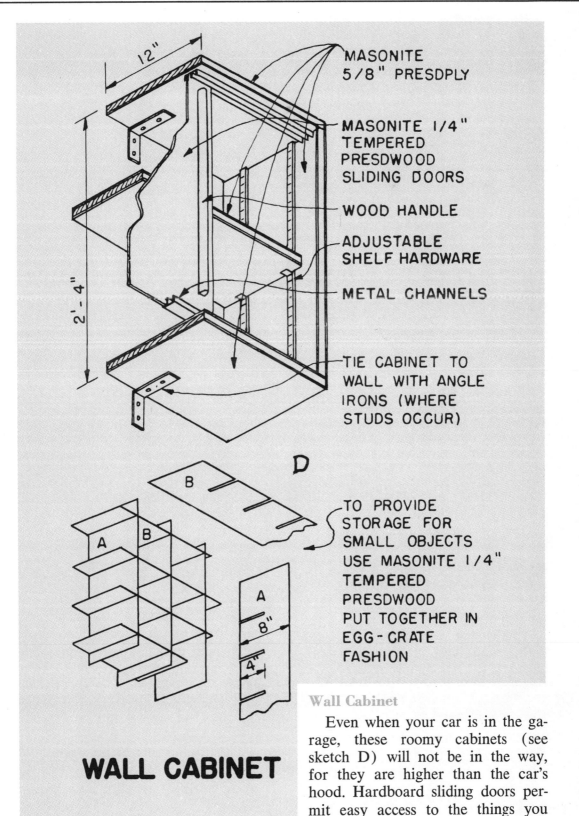

12"

MASONITE
5/8" PRESDPLY

MASONITE 1/4"
TEMPERED
PRESDWOOD
SLIDING DOORS

WOOD HANDLE

ADJUSTABLE
SHELF HARDWARE

METAL CHANNELS

2'- 4"

TIE CABINET TO
WALL WITH ANGLE
IRONS (WHERE
STUDS OCCUR)

D

B

TO PROVIDE
STORAGE FOR
SMALL OBJECTS
USE MASONITE 1/4"
TEMPERED
PRESDWOOD
PUT TOGETHER IN
EGG-CRATE
FASHION

A   B

A

A

8"

4"

WALL CABINET

Wall Cabinet

Even when your car is in the garage, these roomy cabinets (see sketch D) will not be in the way, for they are higher than the car's hood. Hardboard sliding doors permit easy access to the things you

Materials Needed

STORAGE PLATFORM			WORKTABLE		
80 sq. ft.	hardboard	⅛" thick	1 panel	¾" hard-board	2'-6"x5'-4"
8 pcs.	fir	2x4x8'	3	hinges	
80 sq. ft.	wood deck-ing	1x6	6	eye hooks	
24	metal straps	18" long	10'	link chain	
			2	chain snaps	
WALL CABINETS					
1 panel	¾" hard-board	4'x8'	**CORNER CABINETS**		
1 panel	¼" hard-board	4'x8'	3 panels	¼" hard-board (use remain-ders for egg-crate shelv-ing in wall cabinets)	4'x8'
8	angle irons				
16'	metal chan-nels for slid-ing doors		1	angle iron	
4	adjustable shelf standards	2'	8 pcs.	fir for cabi-net frame	2x4x8'
8	adjustable shelf brack-ets		5 pcs.	white pine for door	1⅛"x2"x8'
1 pc.	clear white pine (for door han-dles)	½"x1"x8'	1	door handle and latch	
			4 prs.	butt hinges	3"x3"
			2	robe hooks	

keep on the plywood shelving.

Cabinets should be built first, following sketch carefully. Then they are mounted in position on the wall which serves as the back of the cabinet, using angle irons securely fastened to the studding.

The sketch also shows how to build small bins out of ¼" hardboard. Saw kerfs should be ¼" wide to admit other part of "egg-crate."

Corner Cabinet

Here is a cabinet to solve the problem of where to keep your lawn mower so it's out of the way and to give you a place to hang up your work clothing (see sketch E). You can even attach a padlock to the door if desired. The side and back framework need not be covered, if cabinet is applied over wall paneling.

Conditioning Instructions

Before applying hardboard and perforated panels in a garage, scrub cold water into the screen side with a stiff broom until the panels turn a dark chocolate-brown color. Cover with damp newspaper or tarpaulin and allow to remain for at least 24 hours. Apply while still in moist condition. This will assure the presence of adequate moisture in the board and will eliminate the possibility of expansion.

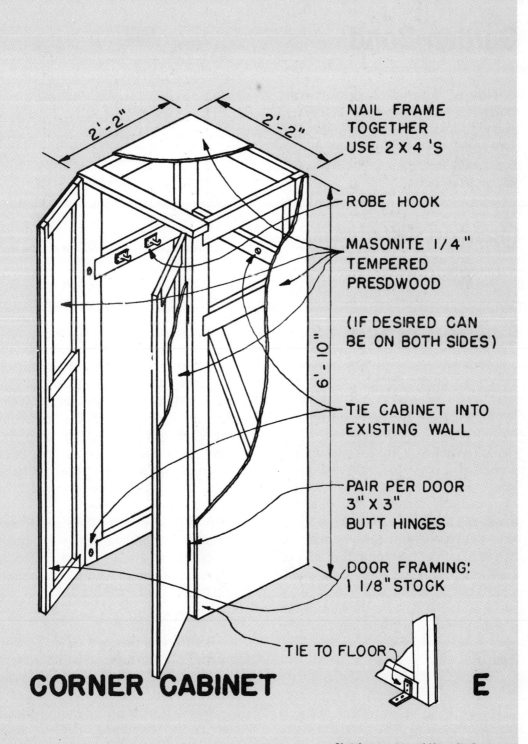

2'-2"

2'-2"

NAIL FRAME
TOGETHER
USE 2 X 4 'S

ROBE HOOK

MASONITE 1/4"
TEMPERED
PRESDWOOD

(IF DESIRED CAN
BE ON BOTH SIDES)

6'-10"

TIE CABINET INTO
EXISTING WALL

PAIR PER DOOR
3" X 3"
BUTT HINGES

DOOR FRAMING:
1 1/8" STOCK

TIE TO FLOOR

CORNER CABINET

E

Sketches courtesy of Masonite Corp.

Garden Bond

This is a form of brick laying which consists of three stretchers in every course followed by a header. There are several variations of this bond with a header set between two to five stretchers.

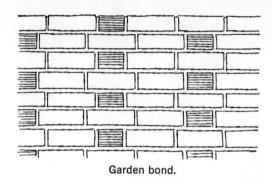

Garden bond.

Garden Furniture

For plans and how to care for garden furniture, see *OUTDOOR FURNITURE*.

Garden Hose

Daily care of the hose, during the season when it is being used, is essential. When you finish watering the garden it is best to drain the hose. Never fold a hose when it's not in use; instead, it must be coiled to avoid any strain at a fold which could lead to eventual cracking or tearing. Never hang the hose on a thin nail or hook, as that might produce a weakened spot which could result in a crack. A reel is best for the hose when it's not in use; you could buy or make one. Always store the hose in a dry spot.

Mending a Small Leak

If the leak in a rubber hose is small, clean and wipe dry the damaged spot; then squeeze on to it a thick coat of rubber-base cement, which you buy in a tube. Let it dry for about 10 minutes, then put on a second thin coat of the cement. Wind friction tape around the cemented part. For a minute or two keep your hand over the tape, to make it stick. Then permit it to dry thoroughly before using the hose for watering again.

A plastic hose with a small leak cannot be handled this way; but it must be repaired in the following manner, which is also recommended for big leaks in a rubber hose.

Splicer and Mending Tube

Before you proceed with the work on the plastic hose, dip the ends in hot water to soften the plastic and make it more flexible.

Whether you are mending plastic or badly damaged rubber hose, the first thing to do is to cut away the damaged portion with a sharp

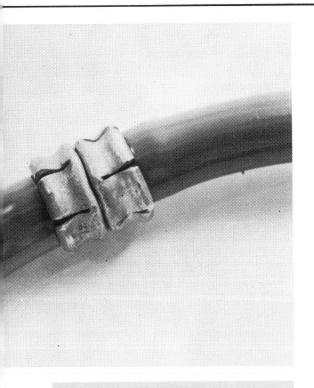

A hose splicer is used to join two sections of hose after the piece which had a hole or tear is cut away. The prongs are forced inward to grip the hose wall.

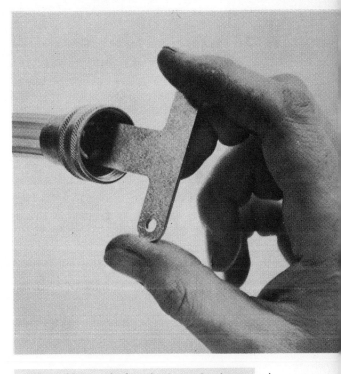

When either end of a plastic garden hose has to be replaced, you can use a special type of coupling with a threaded wedge unit inside the hose. This unit is turned or tightened with a special key and forms a leak-free union.

knife. Making straight cuts to insure no jagged ends. At the hardware or garden supply store you can buy a metal splicer or a mending tube with pipe clamps, which are made for the purpose of hose repairs.

To use a splicer, insert one end flush into the hose. Slowly tap each prong at a time, until all are set into the hose firmly with a tight grip. Then into the other end of the hose insert the other end of the splicer, and again working carefully and slowly, tap the prongs for firmness and tight grip.

To use the mender tube, insert the tube into one end of the hose, then put a pipe clamp onto the hose and slide it ½″ in from the edge of the hose. Now tighten the bolt and nut on the clamp with a screwdriver to make it secure. Onto the other end of the hose put the second pipe clamp; then insert the mender tube into the hose; now the two hose ends meet (over the mender tube which is inside). Slide the clamp over to about 1″ from the first clamp; then tighten the bolt and nut on this second clamp.

Also see *HOSE COUPLINGS.*

Garden Tools

Every spring, millions of home-owners yank out their garden tools and get to work. Some, however, have to stop because their tools are not in shape. They failed to take care of their garden tools before they put them away for the winter. Here is a guide for the proper care of your garden tools:

1. Remove all the dirt and any rust that might be on the tool. You can use a wire brush for the surface cleaning. If there are stubborn rust spots, use a rust remover, such as ammonium citrate available at drug stores.

2. Sharpen all cutting tools. Use a file or a whetstone for the job. See *Sharpening*.

3. Check the handles to see if they are tight. Should the handle be loose, it's necessary to repair it at once. If the handle comes off, use adhesive and set it back on.

4. While checking the handle, if it is made of wood, examine it for signs of splits. If there is a split, apply adhesive and clamps; see *ADHESIVES* and *CLAMPS*.

5. If the wood is rough, use sandpaper to get it smooth again.

Here are several of the more popular hand tools for the garden enthusiast: (1) trowel, (2) transplanting trowel, (3) cultivator-hoe, (4) midget rake, (5) midget cultivator, (6) combination cultivator-weeder, (7) cultivator-spade combination, (8) midget fork, (9) cultivator-tweezer, (10) steel hand broom, (11) dandelion cutter, (12) dibble and (13) hollow planter.

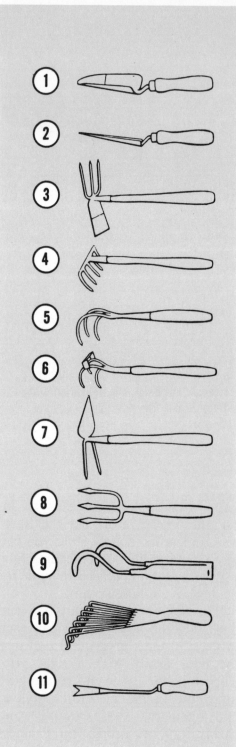

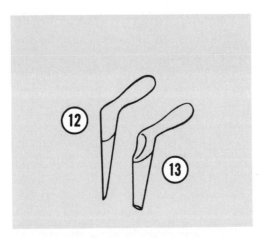

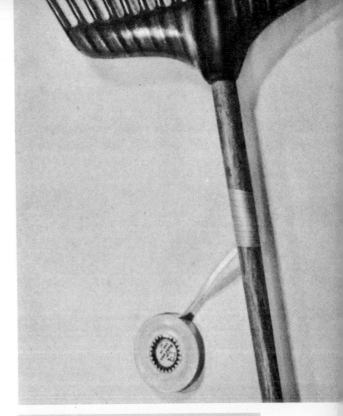

6. Apply a coat of varnish to the wood handles, or rub with an oily rag. They will last longer if you do.

7. Coat all metal parts with oil, grease or varnish so that the tools remain rust-free during the winter.

8. Store all tools safely in a dry place where they will be out of the way for the winter months. Protect all cutting edges by covering with cardboard taped to the metal or several layers of masking tape over the sharp edge.

9. Check your lawn mower. Clean it and sharpen it before you put it away for the season.

10. If you have a power mower, it is necessary to put the motor to "bed" for the winter.

See *MOWERS, SPRAYERS* and *SPRINKLERS*.

A small, slight crack in a wooden handle can be repaired by wrapping the handle with tape. A glass filament tape is particularly useful for such a job.

If part of the tool is loose, separate it. Then glue it together with a water-proof adhesive. See section on Adhesives.

Types of Garden Tools

The ardent gardener has almost as many tools as the hobbyist in his workshop. Many are special tools designed for a specific job; they do that job best and should be used if you wish to get the best results. Of course, if you need the tool for a short time only, you can usually find another tool that you already have to take its place.

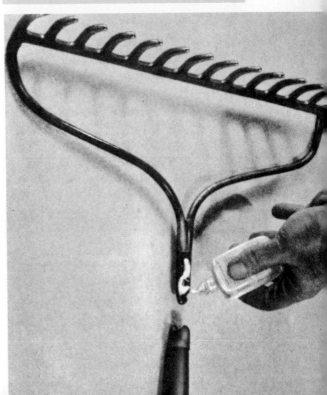

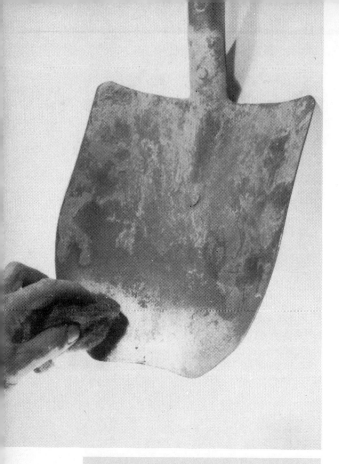

Remove all caked earth from the metal surfaces of all garden tools. Use a wire brush to remove the top surface and then scrub with steel wool.

Tools, Care and Repair

Knowing how to use the garden tools will do much to prevent personal injury. For example, properly uncoiling a hose will prevent you from tripping or catching your foot in the coil. The points of an upturned rake can inflict painful and sometimes serious puncture wounds when stepped on, to say nothing about the possibility of the handle flying up and striking you in the face. Tools must not be left where their edges or point may be hidden by grass, leaves, or other material. Keep your fingers away from the blades of the lawn mower; merely striking your hand against the blades while oiling, cleaning, or adjusting them, may re-sult in painful injury if you catch your fingers between the revolving and stationary blades.

The handles of all tools should be free of cracks and splinters, and strong enough not to break under ordinary usage. A tool doesn't need to be discarded because of a handle break; you can buy a new handle at the hardware store or make a new handle yourself and attach it to the tool.

If the handle splits but doesn't break, repair it by winding wire or cord around the split part, then cover it with tape, or you can use bolts.

Splintering and roughness of a wood handle may be remedied by

A turf edger makes for a well-groomed lawn. It works around trees, walks, curves, circular beds and along driveways.
Photograph courtesy of Gardex Tools.

Photograph courtesy of Homko Tools,
Western Tool & Stamping Co.

An electric edger does the same job but a motor does the "work."

sanding the surface until it becomes smooth again; this not only protects your hands, but keeps the cracks from spreading and causing the handle to break.

A good way to preserve a wood handle is to apply several coats of quality varnish or to paint it. The metal parts of the tool may be painted, with a primer coat of red lead, and two coats of exterior paint. However, any metal part which goes into the ground should not be painted. Aside from preservation by paint, the tools are easier to find when their handles are of a color which makes them conspicuous if left lying on the grass; the color, therefore, should not be green or brown, but a bright contrast to the grass such as red, yellow, blue, or white.

The metal edges of shovels, hoes, rakes or other garden tools may become nicked. These may be smoothed with a metal file. Any rough surfaces should be gone over with steel wool or other abrasive which is good for metal. Dents may be straightened out by hammering with a mallet.

A wheelbarrow break, in the wood or metal parts, should be repaired at once. Painting the wheelbarrow helps preserve the wood. The moving part needs occasional oiling, to run smoothly.

For winter storage, keep tools in a dry spot as dampness could be harmful. Wipe all tools clean of any dirt or grass before being stored. The metal parts should be coated with a mixture of petroleum jelly and light oil, to prevent rust.

Gardening, Indoor

You can have growing plants all through the year in your home, even during the winter months if they get sunlight from a bright window and are watered regularly.

Light Required

The rate of growth and the length of time the plant remains in good condition in the home is largely dependent upon the intensity of the light it receives, for light is a source of energy for the production of food. Most plants thrive in full sunlight throughout the year, and only a few should be shaded from the sun during the brightest part of the day. Because some plants grow in less light than do others, one should consider this in selecting a plant for a special place, that is, whether the plant is to be in an east, west, north, or south window.

In a house not shaded by trees, porch, or other objects, and in windows of the same size, either an east, west, or south window is good. The north window would supply as much light in summer as would any other in winter. Trees and other obstacles often render a south window inferior to an unshaded north window. Draperies, shades, and curtains reduce the intensity of light, and seldom are any two windows in the same house alike in light conditions.

Most of the flowering plants require sunlight for satisfactory growth; they should be obtained in full bloom

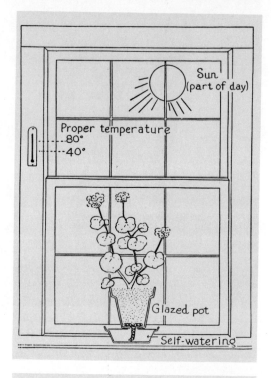

Sun part of the day, proper temperature, plant moisture are essential for ample growth.

or well-budded and allowed to open in the home. Many foliage plants grow well where the light is only bright enough to permit reading most of the day.

In the home the three intensities of light for the growth of plants are: (1) *sun* part of the day, which is best for nearly all the flowering plants; (2) *bright light,* which is just out of the sun or in the unshaded north window, suitable for plants that flower for a short time or for ferns and many foliage plants; and (3) *shade,* which is light of enough intensity to read by most of the day, suitable for sansevieria, palms, peperomias, philodendron, and a few others.

Bright, artificial light keeps many plants alive a longer time than if they were kept in the dark; to be most effective, it should shine on the plant at least ten hours each day. Plants in poorly lighted positions have to be replaced frequently.

Temperature

The best night temperature for all plants is between 50° and 60° F. The length of life of a flowering plant is reduced by high night temperature regardless of other conditions. A plant in bright light during the day may be given a night temperature near 70° F., but one in poor light needs a lower temperature. A plant near the window is cooler than one far from it, because of the radiation of heat from the plant to the cool glass. It is well to remove plants from a warm room to a cool place at night.

Probably temperature fluctuations in the home are of little importance if the range is between 40° and 80° F. and if the temperature at night is lower than that during the day.

Wick watering.

Ventilation

Plants in light remove carbon dioxide from air and put oxygen into it. At night they give off some carbon dioxide, but so little that it is of no importance. Plants need not be removed from the bedroom or sickroom at night to assure the health of the patient; for if an entire plant were converted to carbon dioxide, the amount produced would be of no importance. Usually the patient's room is cooler than the room to which the plants are taken; consequently they fade earlier by such treatment.

Ventilation reduces the concentration of any illuminating gas that may be present. Illuminating gas usually causes the lower leaves of plants to turn yellow and drop.

Artificial or coal gas can be detected in the home by bringing freshly cut carnations into the room. The petals close upward, "go to sleep," in from six to ten hours when gas is present. One cannot detect natural gas by this method, but it causes the plants to harden, lose their leaves, and to stop growth. Plants are affected by gas long before humans detect it. One should take every precaution to prevent its escape into the room. If it does escape into the home, perhaps the piping in the house is faulty or the gas main in the street may be leaking.

Plants should never be placed where air blows over them freely, such as over a radiator, in front of a fan, or in an open window. The loss of water in such a position is greater than the roots can supply and the plants may wilt.

Fertilizer

Fertilizer does not offset the effects of poor light, high temperature, or other factors causing poor growth. It seldom benefits a sick plant, and over-fertilization may kill plants.

A mature plant obtained from a florist requires no fertilizer for at least six weeks and usually needs none for a longer period. Other plants growing in the home generally require an application of fertilizer only three or four times each year.

A mixed fertilizer of a 4-12-4 or 5-10-5 analysis may be used at the rate of a teaspoonful to a pot 5″ in diameter. It can be watered into the soil after its application. Patented fertilizers in tablet, powder, or liquid form are more expensive but are satisfactory. If no commercial fertilizer is available for use on house plants, it is probably best to remove the plant from the pot and repot it in the same container. Use newly prepared soil to replace that removed from the top and bottom of the ball.

Tea, coffee, castor oil, and other remedies and stimulants are of no value other than for the small amounts of fertilizer they supply.

Usually, soil acidity needs no consideration except for such plants as hydrangea, azalea, and gardenia, which require acid soil.

Flowering Plants

You can grow flowering plants in a window that receives the morning sun and is not shaded.

The African violet is especially easy to grow because you can start with a leaf and a small piece of stem

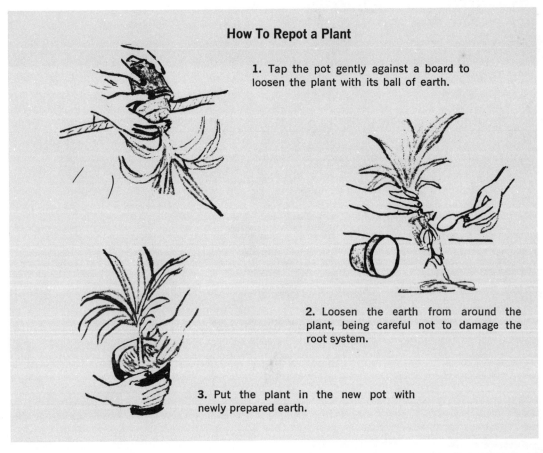

How To Repot a Plant

1. Tap the pot gently against a board to loosen the plant with its ball of earth.

2. Loosen the earth from around the plant, being careful not to damage the root system.

3. Put the plant in the new pot with newly prepared earth.

attached to it. Root this in a pot in sand. Pot it in soil as soon as it has rooted. Do not let the room get colder than 60° F., and be sure to keep the soil moist. The plant will have beautiful blue flowers after about 4 months.

Perhaps you can get a small shoot from a Christmas cactus. It produces deep pink flowers from the edges of the leaves. Flowers first appear soon after Christmas, and new ones keep opening until Easter. Keep the plant watered during the summer and it will flower again the next year.

Take a shoot from a geranium plant in September and root it in a pot or in a glass of water in the window. Pot it in soil after it roots.

Pinch the tip from it when two or three new leaves have formed. Pinching causes the plant to branch and to produce a bushy plant. Geraniums grow best in a south window.

Bulbous Plants

You can grow several different kinds of bulbous plants.

Paper white narcissi bulbs can be purchased in October. Plant them in gravel, soil, or what you have handy, and keep water in the container. Put them in a sunny window and your reward will be a cluster of pearly white flowers in December.

The amaryllis bulb can be purchased in January. This should be potted in soil. The flower bud starts

One method of storing bulbs and tubers is to pack them in vermiculite. This granular mineral will protect them against freezing, against rapid fluctuations in temperature, and excess moisture. A spongy material, vermiculite takes up moisture that may collect on the bulbs, but does not absorb their normal, internal moisture. The container should be put in the coolest place in the house but not where the temperature is apt to drop below 32°. A basement, fruit cellar, or utility room is generally a good location.

immediately and produces large pink, red, or white lily-like flowers before the leaves are full-grown. Be careful not to plant the bulb more than two-thirds under the soil. Keep it growing after it flowers. Keep the plant growing through the summer, and it will flower the next year.

The gloxinia bulb-like structure can be planted during April. It sends forth leaves and velvety flowers, the shape of large morning-glories. Put it in a window where it gets the morning sun. It is best watered with a wick.

Hardy Bulbs

Tulips, narcissi, crocuses, snow-drops, and all the other hardy bulbs flower in the house during January, February, and March. Pot the bulbs in October and store them in the basement with the potatoes. Be sure to water them once each week or more often if they need it. If the basement is not cool, store them outdoors in a pit.

Bring potted bulbs into the house

in January and watch them stretch and flower in a sunny window.

Non-Flowering Plants

Grow plants that do not flower if you have no sunny windows. They grow best where they get good light and some sun, but will grow with no sun.

You can start a showy-leaved begonia from a leaf cutting. Sometimes they flower, but the leaves are most interesting. You can grow them in a north window.

Just put a piece of baby's tears in soil in a shallow dish and keep it very moist by setting the container in a shallow saucer with water. Do not let it stay in the sun.

A small Boston fern soon outgrows a small pot and must be transplanted. Grow it in a window where it gets some sun. New plants come from runners, as do strawberry plants.

You can grow Chinese water evergreen in a dish of water or in soil. The sun does not have to shine directly on the leaves.

Potted plant soil can be kept properly aerated by removing the soil, mixing it with vermiculite, then repotting. The granular mineral keeps the soil light and airy, prevents it from compacting or caking, and helps provide sufficient water and air to the plant roots. One part by volume of vermiculite mixed well with two parts of soil is the recommended mixture.

Root in a dish of water a piece of English ivy from an older plant. Pot it in soil after it roots. It grows best in a window where it gets a little sun.

Use a 4″ to 5″ piece of philodendron and root it in a glass of water. Put it in soil after it roots. Philodendron needs no sunlight.

Additional Indoor Plants

For a more complete list of plants, refer to the section on "Plants for the Home."

How To Water Plants

You will be sure of having the soil just moist enough if you water all your plants with wicks. You can buy wicks of spun glass or you may make them from burlap. If you make them from burlap, renew them every two months because they rot. Take a piece of burlap 5″ long and tie it in several places. Cut one end down from the top 1½″ and flare the top. Push the tied end through the hole from the inside of the flower pot. Flatten the untied end on the inside bottom of the flower pot. Put soil or sand in the pot and no coarse material. Set the flower pot on a second container which has water in it all the time. The wick works like a lamp wick pulling water into the soil.

Flower Boxes

For information on boxes in the house and on window sills, refer to section on *FLOWER BOXES AND PLANTERS*.

Gardening— Indoor Plants

Photograph courtesy of Armstrong Cork Co.

UPRIGHT-FOLIAGE PLANTS

Air Plant or Life Plant (kalanchoe or Bryophyllum) grows in bright light or sun. Propagation is by the young plants that form on the edge of the leaf. One kind has flat leaves and another has tubular leaves.

Aloe grows in full sun or shade and doesn't need too much water. Propagation is by small shoots that form near the base of the plant.

Anthericum grows in bright light. Propagation is by young plants that form on the stems.

Boston Fern (nephrolepis) grows best in bright light. Propagation is by runners that form new plants when they strike the soil.

Cacti grow in full sun or shade. A sandy soil and not too much water are best. Propagation is by seeds or cutting. (Refer to *Christmas Cactus*).

Caladiums require bright light and a uniformly moist soil. Propagation is by division of tubers.

Cast Iron Plant (Aspidistra) grows under any conditions. Propagation is by division.

Century Plant (Agave) requires sun or shade and not too much water. Propagation is by cuttings of the small shoots near the base.

Chinese Water Evergreens (Aglaonema) grows well in shade, in soil or water, and in any soil moisture. Propagation is by cuttings rooted in water or sand.

Coleus should be grown in sunlight. Propagation is by terminal cuttings. New plants should replace old ones frequently because of the ungainly growth. The plants require pinching to cause branching.

Jade Plant (Crassula) grows in shade or sun. Propagation is by leaf or terminal cuttings.

Maranta is a creeping plant that grows best in bright light or shade in shallow containers. The soil should be kept very moist.

Peperomia should be grown in bright light or shade. Propagation is by terminal cuttings or by leaf-cuttings.

Pick-a-Back Plant (Tolmiea Menziesii) does well in sun or bright light. Propagation is by the young plants that form on the leaves.

Rubber Plants (Ficus), many varieties, grow well in bright or poor light. Propagation is by leaf-bud or terminal cuttings.

Silk Oak (Grevillea) grows in sun or bright light. Propagation is by seeds.

Strawberry Geranium (Saxifraga sarmentosa) grows best in sun or bright light. New plantlets develop on runners.

Velvet Plant (Gynura) does best in bright light. Propagation is by terminal cuttings. The plant requires pinching to cause branching.

FOLIAGE VINES

Asparagus grows best in full sun or partial shade. Propagation is by seeds or division.

Baby's Tears (Helxine) requires bright or poor light and plenty of water, but watering should be done from below rather than from above. The plant should be grown in a shallow container and the base of the container kept in water, or a wick should be used. Propagation is by division.

English Ivies (Hedera Helix), many varieties, grow well in bright light and in very poor light. Propagation is by terminal cuttings.

German Ivy (Senecio Mikanioides) needs sun or bright light. It does poorly in the home because of lack of light; it grows best in a window box outside. Propagation is by leaf-bud or terminal cuttings.

Grape Ivy (Cissus) grows best in bright light but withstands poor light well. Propagation is by leaf-bud or terminal cuttings. Two kinds are available.

Nephthytis does well in bright light or shade, and needs plenty of water. Propagation is by leaf-bud or terminal cuttings.

Periwinkle (Vinca major) is not a good house plant but is good for a window box in sun or shade. Propagation is by leaf-bud or terminal cuttings.

Philodendron can be grown in bright light or poor light. It may be grown in water or dry soil. Propagation is by leaf-bud or terminal cuttings.

Wandering Jew (Tradescantia or Zebrina) grows in sun or bright light. Propagation is by terminal cuttings.

Wax Plant (Hoya carnosa) grows in sun or bright light. Propagation is by leaf-bud or terminal cuttings.

FLOWERING PLANTS

Achimenes can be grown from the cone-like storage root planted during March to May and placed in a sunny window. They flower during summer. After the plant has flowered, the soil

Plants for East or West Windows

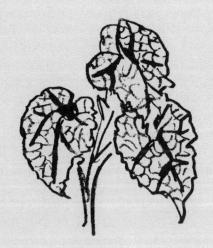

Begonia

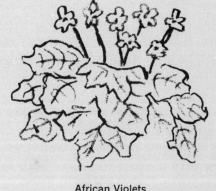

African Violets

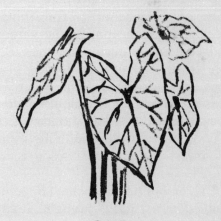

Caladium

Pandamus

should be allowed to dry gradually and then the plant should be stored in a cool, dark place. Before growth starts again the next year, the old soil should be shaken from the roots and replaced by new.

African Violet (Saintpaulia) does not flower in poor light. During summer, it should be placed in bright light; during winter, in sun. It will not endure summer sun. African violet is best watered from below; the wick method is excellent. It can be grown from a leaf-petiole cutting.

Amaryllis (Hippeastrum) bulbs planted about half under soil during November to January flower in early spring. They should be grown in sun. After flowering, they are kept growing in the pot or are planted in a shady place in the garden. They should be protected from frost. They are not allowed to dry.

Astilbe cannot be forced into bloom successfully in the home. Plants in flower obtained from the florist should be watered with a wick or set with the base of the pot in shallow water, and kept in sun or bright light. The plants are hardy and may be planted in the garden after danger of freezing has passed. Propagation is by division.

Azalea (*Rhododendron*) grows in bright light or sun and needs a uniform supply of water. One should buy only plants with many buds and a few open flowers. The buds open in the home. After flowering, the plant may be kept in light where it will grow. After danger of freezing, it may be planted in the pot in the garden and kept moist during summer. Before frost, it should be placed in a cool, well-ventilated room where it does not freeze. A bedroom window is usually good. About January 1, it may be brought into the living room to flower. An acid, peaty soil is required.

Everblooming Begonia (*Begonia semperflorens)* needs sunlight. It can be grown in the window from a cutting from the base of the plant. It may be grown from seeds. It is a good bedding plant.

Calla Begonia (*Begonia semperflorens)* grows in bright light but not sunlight. Propagation is from cuttings only. It is grown primarily for the interesting foliage.

Rex Begonia and all rhizomatous forms grow in bright light but not sunlight, Propagation is by leaf cuttings. They are grown for the foliage.

Christmas Begonia (*Begonia socotrana*) is the most showy of the be-

gonias but the most difficult to grow. It should be purchased with many buds, grown in sun, and discarded after flowering because of the difficulty of growing it in the home.

Tuberous - Rooted Begonias are planted in March in moist soil, grow in sun until May, and then in bright light. After they have finished flowering, the plants should be allowed to dry, and then the tubers placed in sand or dry peat and stored over winter in a cool basement. They may be grown from seeds. They are excellent garden plants in a moist, shaded position.

Miscellaneous Begonias include the better varieties of fibrous-rooted forms. They grow best in sun or bright light and are propagated from terminal cuttings.

Butterfly Flowers or Poor Man's Orchids (*Schizanthus*) should be bought in flower and given full sun or bright light. They are annuals and die after flowering. They should not be grown from seeds in the home.

Calceolaria should be bought with many flowers and buds, kept in sun, and at about 50° F at night. The plant should be discarded after flowering.

Calla (*Zantedeschia*), both the yellow and the white, should be grown in sun and given plenty of water. It is dried off during June and kept as cool as possible until August, when the white-calla corm is replanted in new soil and started into growth again. The yellow calla must be left in a dry condition until November or later. Propagation is by offsets of the fleshy storage organ.

Christmas Cactus (Zygocatus truncatus) grows in sun and where the night temperature during winter is

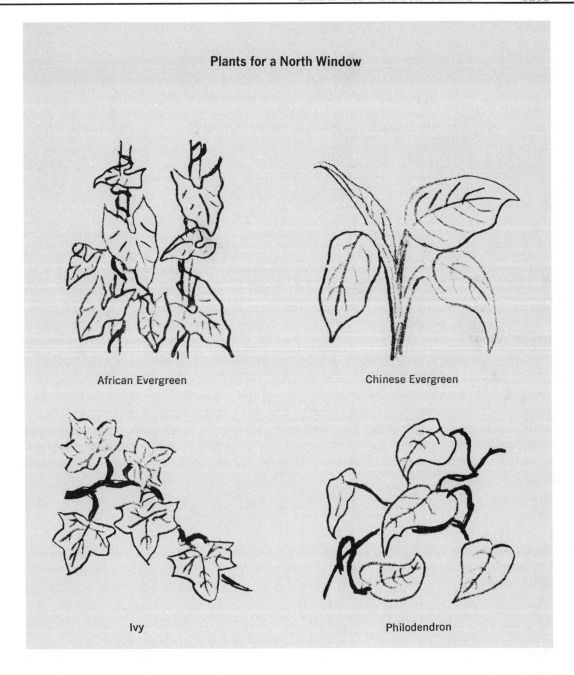

Plants for a North Window

African Evergreen

Chinese Evergreen

Ivy

Philodendron

from 60° to 65° F. It should not be kept dry like other cacti and does especially well if the soil is always moist. Flower buds start during October, and the plant will continue to flower during winter and spring. Bud drop occurs when the temperature is too high or the light intensity too low.

planted during June or July and the It can be grown out of doors in summer.

Christmas Pepper (Capsicum Frutescens) should be bought in full fruit and discarded after it loses its value as an ornamental because it is an annual. It can be grown from seed seedlings grown in pots in the garden. (See *Jerusalem Cherry*.)

Chrysanthemum plants in the garden may be dug and potted during August to be flowered in the house. They should be kept out of doors as long as possible. They need sun. The varieties obtained from the florist are usually not hardy and may as well be discarded after flowering.

Cineraria should be obtained with buds and flowers, kept in sun, and placed in a room at about 50° F at night. The plant should be discarded after flowering.

Citrus plants grow well in sun if given a good supply of water. They can be propagated from seeds or cuttings.

Cyclamen should be obtained with many flowers and placed in sun at a cool (50° F.) night temperature. The leaves turn yellow and the buds blast if the temperature is too high or the light intensity too low.

After the plant has flowered, the soil may be kept dry until June, when the corm can be removed and planted in new soil and to grow the next year. In a cool bright window, the plant usually flowers again.

Easter Lily needs sun. The bulbs may be planted before Christmas and the plants will flower in the home, but to obtain a plant well budded and watch the buds open is more satisfactory. The plant should be discarded after flowering.

Fuchsia is not a good house plant unless it can be grown in sun. It is best for garden or window box. Flowering stops in summer because of high temperature. It is propagated from cuttings.

Gardenia should be grown in sun and the night temperature kept near 60° F. The buds drop if these conditions are not maintained. Even though it has no flowers gardenia makes an attractive foliage plant. Propagation is by cuttings.

Genista (*Cytisus*) loses its buds and flowers at a temperature above 60° F. It should not be expected to flower if grown in the home, but makes a good foliage plant. It should be obtained in full bloom.

Geranium (*Pelargonium*) is available in many varieties and some are most valuable for the odor of the foliage. All grow best in sun and all are propagated from cuttings.

Gloxinia (*Sinningia Speciosa*) tubers planted during March or April flower in early summer. They grow and flower well in sun until May, when they should be placed in bright light. They are most satisfactory when watered from below by a wick. After they have flowered the soil can be kept quite dry until the foliage wilts and dies, then the tuber, left in the soil, can be stored in the basement until the following spring when it can be removed from the soil and potted in new soil to start growth again.

Heather (*Erica*) grows in sun or poor light after the buds are nearly open. The soil must be kept especially moist. The plant should be discarded after flowering.

Hydrangea flowers are pink when the soil is slightly acid and blue on the same plant when the soil is very acid. The plant requires much water and grows best in sun and quite well in bright light. After the plant has flowered, the stems should be cut about 2″ above the ground and planted in the garden. The new shoots flower the next year.

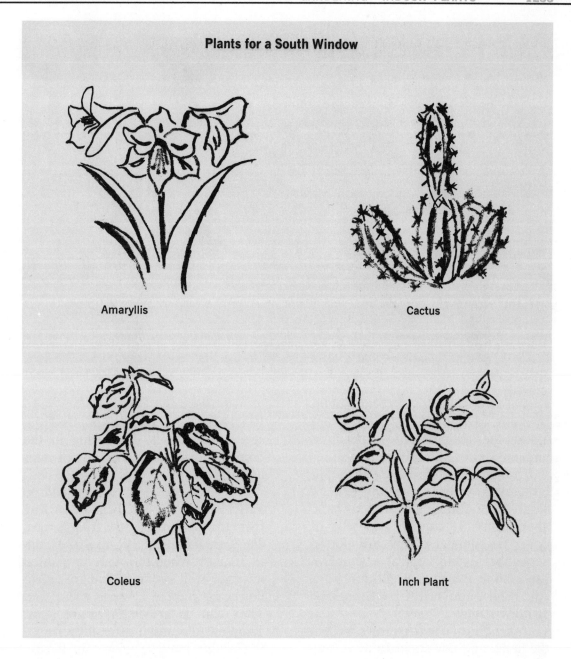

Plants for a South Window

Amaryllis

Cactus

Coleus

Inch Plant

Before September 1 the plant should be dug, potted, and left outdoors in sun until the first light frost. Then it should be stored in a cool, dark place, such as the basement, until January 1, when it can be brought into the living room in a sunny window to grow and flower. The soil must be kept moist in storage as well as during the growing period. Yellow between the veins of the leaves usually is due to an alkaline soil.

Jerusalem Cherry (*Solanum Pseudo-capsicum*) is best obtained from a florist when fruits are mature. They naturally drop soon. It should be kept

Photographs courtesy of Armstrong Cork Co.

as cool as possible and in bright light. It is not advisable to keep the plant for another year because it becomes ungainly and seldom flowers well.

If it is to be carried over, it should be kept growing in sun and pruned severely to obtain the proper shape about May. It can be kept out of doors in summer. They are potted September 1 and kept at a temperature above freezing, preferably in a cold-frame, until near Christmas. (See also *Christmas Pepper*.)

Kafier-Lily (*Clivia*) grows well in the home and flowers in June. It may be kept in the same pot for years. It should be kept cool and in good light during winter, and placed in the garden in a pot during summer. Propagation is by division.

Kalanchoe (Kalanchoe Blossfeldiana) is obtained in bud or bloom and kept in sun or bright light. After flowering, it can be continued in growth and may flower another year. It is best to start new plants from seeds or cuttings. Flowering in the home is questionable because of poor light.

Lily - of - the - Valley (Convallaria majalis) pips (rootstocks) are dug from the garden after the foliage dies. They are stored at 30° to 40° F. until January when they can be planted in sand, soil, or moss and forced to flower by merely keeping them wet. They can be grown in bright light. They are discarded after flowering.

Orchids may be grown in a case where the humidity can be kept high, but it is more satisfactory to purchase plants with buds ready to open and let them open in the home. After flowering they are best returned to the greenhouse where better care can be given than in the home. They grow better in sun or bright light. The flowers last several weeks.

Poinsettias (*Euphorbia pulcherrima*) are best obtained in full bloom, grown in sun, and discarded after Christmas. They seldom flower in the home because of the high temperature and the poor light. If one cares to grow them a second year, the soil is dried after flowering and the plants are stored in a cool room. They are cut to 5″ or 6″ from the ground in May and allowed to grow again. They may be planted in pots in the garden in summer and taken into the home September 1. Leaf drop is caused by poor light, high temperature, or improper watering.

Primulas grow in sun and a cool night temperature. The plants are discarded after flowering. They are difficult to continue in growth during summer.

Roses need sun and plenty of moisture. After flowering, the plant should be kept in sun and grown until it can be planted permanently in the garden. They are hardy.

Shrimp Plant (Beloperone guttata) grows in bright light. New plants are produced from cuttings.

Slipperwort (*Calceolaria*) is purchased in bloom or with blooms and many buds. It is kept in sun, and discarded after flowering. The foliage yellows if the light is poor.

Snapweed (*Impatiens*) is grown in sun in winter. Its best use is in a window box in shade or in a shady spot in the garden. Propagation is by cuttings.

Bulbs For Forcing

Tulips, narcissi, hyacinths, and other hardy bulbs can be planted in pots in September or October and kept in a cool basement at about 40° to 50° F. to January, when they can be brought to the living-room window and made to flower. The soil must be kept moist in storage. The plants grow in sun. After the plant has flowered, the foliage should be allowed to grow until it turns yellow when the soil can be dried and the bulbs later planted in the garden. One should not attempt to force the same bulbs in two successive years.

Paper-White narcissi bulbs should be planted in pebbles or soil and placed directly in the sun in the living room. Cold treatment before forcing is of little value.

Garnet Paper

Garnet paper is used for sanding. It is a paper covered with a reddish abrasive, which is fairly hard.

Garnet paper is used for hand finishing of hardwood and softwood as well as composition board and cork.

Also see *ABRASIVES*.

Gas Appliances

The selection of the appliances with which gas is used is much more important than is commonly supposed. The American Gas Association, a national organization, has established a laboratory for determining whether appliances offered for sale are so designed that they can be used safely and with satisfaction. Specifications called "approval requirements," with which an appliance must comply before it can be regarded as safe, have been adopted. To receive the approval of the Association, an appliance must pass a number of careful tests. An appliance, whether manufactured by a member of the Association or not, may be submitted for test; and the great majority of models of domestic appliances have been tested. Several thousand models have been approved.

All appliances so approved bear the blue approval star of the Association, and this label is the only certain means available to the average purchaser for distinguishing a safe appliance.

Selecting Appliances

In selecting an appliance for use with propane or butane, make certain that it has been approved for that service. There are important differences between appliances for butane and for manufactured gas, and an appliance made for use with one of them cannot ordinarily be used satisfactorily with the other. In many cases different burners are supplied for manufactured and natural gas. Make sure through the appliance dealer or the manufacturer that you have the right burner.

Even among "approved" appliances which are supposed to be duplicates of the one tested, there may be individual differences or defects which can be distinguished by a well-informed purchaser. Consequently, it is desirable, before accepting a new appliance, to observe it carefully while it is operated under all the conditions likely to exist in service.

There may be difficulties connected with ignition and the uniformity of size and action of the burner "ports," the openings at which the gas burns. All the ports should be clean cut and, unless obviously intended to be different, they should be of uniform size and regularly spaced. Any breaking away, even of the surface, of the original casting around a port should subject the burner to rejection. The gas should ignite without delay at all the ports. The flames at all the ports should be of as nearly uniform size and appearance as the eye can detect. When the air shutter is wide open and the flow of gas is varied as much as possible without extinguishing the flame, the flames at the different ports should remain alike in appearance. There should be no noticeable tendency for any flames to flicker, and if the gas rate can be increased until the flames rise from the ports they should all "lift" at about the same rate.

The difficuty of igniting the gas, if any, and the action of pilot lights and accessory controls such as the safety pilots are readily observed. The purchaser of an appliance should make sure that they are fully understood and entirely satisfactory. Uncertain, partial, or delayed ignition of burners followed by explosion or flashback are the conditions to be guarded against, and considerable differences are to be found even among approved appliances.

Installation

The installation of gas appliances should generally be entrusted only to the gas company or a gas fitter of recognized ability. But the householder should make sure that it is so located that it is easy to use. When the appliance is awkward or difficult to operate, accidents are more likely to occur, Appliances should be so located that they are not subject to excessive drafts which might extinguish the flame. There should be no danger of bumping into or stumbling over

Photo courtesy Caloric Corp.

them or their connections even in the dark. Valves should not be placed where they could be opened by catching clothing on them, where they cannot be easily reached when lighting the gas, not in such a position that a person turning on the gas is forced to stand too near the burner to be safe in case there is a slight explosion. Valves controlling different appliances should be placed far apart if possible. If near together, they should be supplied with handles of such different shapes or material that they can be certainly identified by touch.

Location of appliances in small confined spaces is bad practice; and in extreme cases, for example, where a large water heater is placed in an unventilated closet, the flame may actually be smothered by exhaustion of the oxygen in the air. It is considered dangerous practice to put water

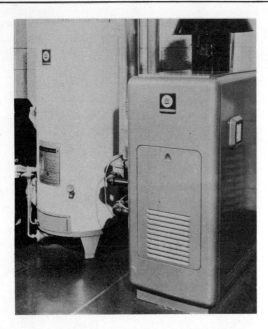

heaters of any kind in bathrooms or bedrooms, or to use heating appliances which discharge the products of combustion into a room in which people sleep. If a bathroom must be heated by an unvented heater, a window or door should be left partly open for ventilation.

In the installation of appliances care must always be taken to avoid any danger of fire. Gas appliances are, in general, much more easily installed properly to safeguard wood floors and walls and other parts of the house or its furnishings than are coal or wood-burning stoves and this has led to a carelessness with gas appliances that is often serious. The risk of fire may be greatly increased by neglect of simple and inexpensive precautions.

Wherever heat is produced continuously for a long period of time, the temperature of nearly combustible materials will be raised dangerously unless there is some provision for removing heat from the space between them and the source of heat.

This is equally true whether the heating is done with a solid fuel, electricity, or gas. Usually the transfer of heat is by convection of the air between the stove or appliance and the floor, partition, or other combustible material, but in recent years many appliances have been designed to be used safely when built into or placed snugly in contact with floors and walls even though they are of wood. In every such case, however, a space has been provided within the appliance itself through which cold air circulates and isolates the region of higher temperature. No reasonable amount of "insulating material" will take the place of the free air space. Failure to understand this is the usual cause of fires from gas-burning appliances.

All appliances which receive the approval of the American Gas Association must pass a test which demonstrates that when they are set 6″ from a wooden wall the wall will not be heated to an unsafe temperature. These appliances designed to be built into or set directly against the wall must pass a corresponding test before approval. Unless the appliance is specifically labeled as approved for flush installation, a 6″ space should be left in every case. This applies to lath-and-plaster walls no less than to wooden partitions.

If any appliance must be placed so close to the floor or wall that after long operation the wood or plaster becomes too hot to be comfortably touched with the hand, additional precautions should be taken. Interposing a sheet of metal or asbestos is usually effective, the more so if it is near to or against the appliance rather than the wall.

Floor furnaces and wall heaters must be installed in such a way that every provision made for the circulation of air is fully effective. Stopping any of the vent holes or reducing the clearances provided for are almost certain to result in disaster.

Wooden shelves should not be placed above a stove or heater; but if this is unavoidable they should be carefully protected on the under side from the heat. Such shelves are particularly dangerous if covered with paper.

Curtains hanging too near gas burners, especially gas lighting fixtures, have been a frequent cause of fire.

In many houesholds, spaces behind and around the appliances are used for the storage of brooms, mops, buckets, cloths, and such household necessities. This should not be done, since it is extremely easy for these articles to be set afire.

Adjustment of Appliances

The possible liberation of carbon monoxide from an appliance in which gas is burning presents a problem distinct from that of raw unburned gas which leaks from pipes or burners. In a gas flame to which there is an unrestricted access of fresh air and no sudden chilling, the carbon monoxide is completely burned. When the flame is partially inclosed and brought into contact with an object which takes away some of the heat, the carbon monoxide may not be completely burned.

It is not always easy to tell when an appliance is liberating carbon monoxide through incomplete combustion, but certain things may well be regarded as warnings. Any odor which does not come from grease, varnish, or other material about the flame to which the odor can be definitely ascribed is a cause for suspicion. Of course, carbon monoxide has no odor; but when any odorous substance is liberated from the flame it is pretty safe to assume that carbon monoxide is liberated too. The usual odor accompanying the liberation of carbon monoxide is slightly irritating to the membranes of the nose but is not particularly unpleasant when not too strong. Many people will identify the odor at once as that given off by a plumber's gasoline torch. It has no resemblance to the odor of the unburned gas. Unfortunately, the absence of any odor is not a positive indication that carbon monoxide is not being liberated, even in dangerous quantity.

Another valuable indication is the appearance of the flame. When a flame has a sufficient supply of fresh air its outlines are sharply defined. When, however, the burning gas is surrounded by an atmosphere from which most of the oxygen has already been used, the outlines of the flames are very faint and indefinite and have a wavering or ragged appearance even in the absence of any noticeable air currents.

Most appliances, when correctly adjusted, have flames with distinct greenish "inner cones," the size of which may be a valuable guide to an adjuster familiar with the particular model with which he is concerned; but the inner cones are of little significance, in general, in judging whether combustion is complete. Carbon monoxide may be liberated in dangerous quantities under certain conditions, from flames with bright, well-formed inner cones, while flames without perceptible inner cones may burn the gas completely. It is the size, form, steadiness, and continuity of the pale blue outer boundary of the visible flame which give valuable indications of the safe or unsafe condition of the appliance.

A flame which is depositing carbon (soot) is not necessarily liberating carbon monoxide, but it is to be regarded with suspicion. When the flame flashes back—that is, when the gas burns inside the ports of the burner—carbon monoxide is almost always liberated in dangerous quantity. This condition is usually recognized at once by a roaring noise and a disagreeable odor. Usually there is a distinct pop when flash-back begins.

Whenever any indication of unsatisfactory combustion is observed, notify the gas company, as in a case of leakage. Many gas companies give free service in correcting conditions of this kind and others make only a small charge.

If an appliance is moved from one community to another, or if the character of the gas supply is materially changed, for example, from manufactured to natural or the reverse, it is particularly important that the appliance be adjusted for the new conditions by an exeprienced man who is entirely familiar with the local situation.

After the adjustment is set, it is dangerous to change it, particularly to enlarge the orifice at a time of low pressure. If service is unsatisfactory because not enough gas is supplied, the trouble may be caused by a partial clogging of the house piping, of the service pipe connecting with the

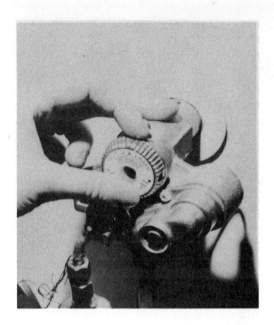

street main, or of the valve controlling the appliance itself; it may be caused by mechanical difficulty in the meter; or it may be the result of a temporary condition which causes low pressure in the mains which supply the neighborhood.

In none of these cases is the enlargement of the orifice a correct or safe method of remedying the trouble. The only safe course is to notify the gas company and permit it to locate and remove the cause of the difficulty.

Although a change of orifice should never be attempted by the average user of gas, an adjustment of the air shutter may usually be made with safety in the case of ranges, water heaters, and some other appliances, but the adjustment of room heaters not directly connected to flues should be left to an expert. Generally, the small flame at each port on the burner should be distinct, free from yellow, and have a sharply defined inner cone. It is not desirable, however, to open the air shutter so wide as to make the flame noisy, to permit flashing back of the flame when turned down as much as it is likely ever to be in use, or to cause any tendency for the flames to "lift" away from the ports.

Operation and Care

In lighting an oven, a water heater, or other appliance in which a large amount of gas is burned in a partially inclosed space, a few simple precautions should be taken to assure safety. Several arrangements for lighting and flame-control exist. In the simplest of them a lighted match is merely applied to the main burner. The match may be brought to a touchhole from which the flame is communicated by a row of small open tube to the burner. A pilot light may be ignited, after which the gas is turned onto the main burner and the pilot light turned off. There may be a pilot light which burns continuously but without a safety pilot; or there may be a safety pilot which, when cold, prevents gas from flowing to the main burner only, or to both the pilot light and the main burner.

In every case the doors of the burner box and oven or of whatever large space communicates with the combustion chamber should be opened first. If a match is to be applied directly to the main burner or to a tube leading from it, the match should be lighted, then the valve should be opened fully and the match brought to the lighting position about one second later. If the lighted match is held over the burner before the valve is opened, the flame is likely to flash back into the explosive mixture formed with the air initially in the burner. If flash-back occurs or if the ignition of the main burner does not occur, close the valve immediately, light another match and try again. If a separately controlled pilot light is provided to assist in the lighting operation, it should be lighted first and the main burner valve opened suddenly. It should then be ascertained that the main burner is actually lighted before turning off the pilot. In case the main burner flashes back when turned on, the gas should be shut off at once and then turned on again before the pilot is extinguished. In case the match flame goes out before the pilot (if any) or the main burner is lighted, the gas should be turned off immediately and another match lighted before the gas is turned on again.

If a safety-pilot is provided which controls the supply of gas to the main burner but not to the pilot, simply light the latter and wait for the safety pilot to warm up and then turn on the main gas supply. When safety-pilot controls the supply of gas to the pilot light as well as to the main burner, instructions as to the lighting of the particular appliance should be obtained from manufacturer or gas company and followed.

In general, the main valve should be opened and heat applied with the flame of a match or taper where it will cause the safety-pilot to open and will ignite the pilot flame. One hand should be on the main burner valve, and another match should be within reach. When the safety-pilot opens, if the gas does not ignite immediately and without flashing back, turn it off at once; then promptly turn it on and apply the match or lighted taper to the main burner as directed for lighting a burner without a pilot. The action must be quick or the safety pilot will cool and again interrupt the gas supply. If failure to light the appliance satisfactorily occurs more than once or twice, the gas company should be asked for advice or assistance.

After lighting but before leaving a burner, the flame should be observed to make sure that perfect ignition has occurred. This applies to burners under the solid or partly inclosed cooking top of a range and to a radiant space heater as much as to an oven, water heater, or furnace.

It sometimes happens that the gas does not light at every port of a burner and unburned gas escapes from those at which there is no flame. Oven burners are especially subject to this trouble. When the gas is lighted, see that there is a flame at every port. If much difficulty is encountered in getting all the ports of the burner to light, something is wrong. Usually the burner needs cleaning, but if cleaning does not remedy the trouble, the burner must be repaired or replaced by an experienced appliance adjuster.

The ignition of flowing sleeves

when women reached over front range burners to light the back ones formerly caused many bad burns. This hazard has been pretty well eliminated by changes in both appliances and clothing but should be kept in mind by women working in the kitchen. The use of catalytic or most friction lighters as a substitute for matches is to be avoided.With such lighters ignition is usually delayed longer than with a match, frequently much longer. Hence, gas may accumulate before ignition to the extent of causing a dangerous flame. The type of friction lighter in which a wheel, rotated by a spring, definitely directs a shower of sparks forward in a narrow stream is the best of these devices and can usually be relied on. It is probably as safe as, or safer than, matches; but the use of many other forms of mechanical or catalytic lighters introduces a distinct hazard.

Appliances should always be kept clean and in good condition. If any part of the appliance appears to be broken, bent, or out of position, you should have an experienced man correct the condition unless the part can be simply replaced, as in the case of the glowers or radiants of radiant heaters.

In all cases safe combustion requires clean burners and unobstructed flue passages. Obstructions in the burner ports or air shutters and accumulations of dirt or soot in the burners modify the design, interfere with the proper mixture of air and gas, and create dangerous conditions. Burners can be easily cleaned by washing in boiling water and soda; they should be dried before using. After cleaning a burner or displacing it for any other reason, it must be carefully restored to exactly its original position.

Nothing is more dangerous than to close the vent of an appliance either by carelessly placing something over it or by deliberately obstructing it, as is sometimes done by persons ignorant of the dangers, for the purpose of saving heat. The proper way to save heat is to burn the gas only when needed and then at the lowest rate that will accomplish the desired work.

A vessel containing a liquid should be closely watched as boiling begins because the liquid may run over the edge of the utensil, extinguish the flame, and permit unburned gas to escape. The boiling over of cooking foods is the most common cause of clogged burners.

Guard against turning a burner too low, for it may blow out or flash back, and thus cause bad results. Especially after a burner has been turned down, one should be sure the flame is actually burning before turning on more gas.

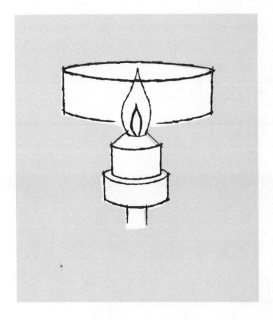

A caution for housewives—keep flammable materials away from the gas range. For example, the range should not be used to dry clothing. Few housewives need to be warned of the danger of overheating deep fat when making doughnuts, fritters, etc., or the paraffin used for sealing jars; but the great concentration of heat in the gas flame and the rapidity with which materials are heated by gas may catch the cook off her guard.

Gas or gasoline is still employed for lighting to some extent in camps and rural homes. The glassware of gas lamps should be maintained in good condition, for not only may glass falling from a broken globe injure someone but also, if highly heated, it may ignite any combustible material on which it falls. Carbon collecting on the mantle because of dirt in, or improper adjustment of, the lamps is also a serious matter; it decreases the amount of light received and hot pieces of the carbon may fall from the lamp and set fire to furnishings. A lamp or any other appliance showing such carbon deposits should be cleaned and adjusted. Mantles should be replaced as soon as the slightest break appears, because the uneven heating resulting from a broken mantle is the usual cause of broken glassware. It is uneconomical as well as unsafe to neglect broken mantles.

Accessories on Appliances

Accessories that may alter the character and size of the flame, or the access of air to the burner and the escape of products of combustion from it, should never be purchased. Particularly to be avoided are the "solid tops" or plates to be placed on a stove designed for the use of a grate top, and the miscellaneous devices sold from house to house and alleged to save gas when placed on other appliances. Meritorious solid top stoves, built as such, are in use but they must be particularly well designed to be safe and reasonably economical. Placing a solid cover on a range not designed for it interferes with the admission of air around the flame and with the escape of the products of combustion through the open grates as intended by the designer.

An attachment which should be strictly avoided is one alleged to filter or purify the gases escaping into the room from an oven or space heater and installed on the vent of the appliance. An open elbow turned away from the wall, or other equivalent deflector, is useful to prevent the streaking of the wall behind an appliance, and may prevent local overheating; but the householder should never allow steel wool or other metallic shavings, perforated plates, or porous material of any kind to be introduced into the vent or flue passages of an appliance.

Flexible Tubing

Considering its limited importance and application, flexible tubing has, without doubt, been the cause of a far greater number of serious accidents than anything else for which there is legitimate use in connection with the burning of gas. Several types of accidents have been common: (a) Cracking or breaking of the tubing itself, allowing gas to escape; (b) the pulling off of the tubing from the appliance or from the gas outlet to which it is connected; (c) the separation of the tubing itself from the connectors which attach it to gas outlet or appliance; (d) the momentary kinking or collapsing of the tubing (when stepped on, for example) which extinguishes the flame or causes it to flash back; and (e) the overheating of the tube or its connectors, which results in leakage.

Burners at which backfiring has occurred usually get extremely hot, and the rubber connectors sometimes melt or burn off. Even the flexible metal tubing with metal connectors usually depends for tightness on a thread of rubber packing and will leak if overheated.

The best precaution against the dangers of flexible tubing is to avoid its use whenever possible. Hot plates, radiant heaters installed in fireplaces, and all other appliances which are to be used in one location for a considerable period of time should always be connected with rigid and permanent piping. There is little difference in cost, considering the fact that the flexible connection may have to be replaced repeatedly during the life of the appliance.

If flexible connections must be used, as in the case of a gas iron, the best tubing obtainable should always be secured. The best available evidence that the tubing is safe is the approval of the American Gas Association, which subjects tubing to a series of rigorous tests to determine its safety from each of the more common hazards. Tubing should always have the connectors at both ends permanently attached at the factory. Always take the utmost care in connecting the tubing. See that the ends are as tight as they can be made and that they will not loosen with a strong

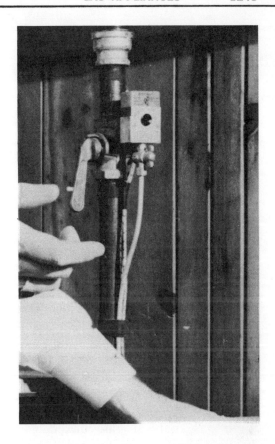

pull. See that no part of the tubing is left in a position in which it may become overheated. The gas should always be shut off the appliance at the inlet end of the tubing, never at the appliance. For this reason it is unsafe to use a flexible tubing with an appliance which has a shut-off.

When tubing which has been in use shows the first sign of leakage or other serious deterioration, throw the piece away and get new tubing. Successful repairs are almost impossible to make. The very best repairs lengthen the life of the tubing so little that the saving effected is negligible. Many deaths have resulted from attempted repairs of this kind.

Also see *GAS HAZARDS*.

Gas Furnace

See *Heating Systems.*

Gas Hazards

Like many other sources of energy, gas must be used carefully, for in careless hands it is a source of great danger. However, nearly all gas accidents are readily preventable by the observance of simple precautions.

Several types of gas are used in American households. The more important of these are commonly classified in the gas industry as manufactured gas, natural gas, mixed gas (natural and manufactured), and liquified petroleum gases (also popularly referred to as bottled gas) which are mainly propane, butane, or their mixtures.

Types of Accidents

In the utilization of gas in the household, five kinds of accidents may occur: (a) Asphyxiation by unburned gas; (b) asphyxiation by the gas resulting from incomplete combustion; (c) burns to persons; (d) destruction of property by fire; and (e) explosions, which may or may not be accompanied by fire or injury to persons.

Asphyxiation by unburned gas occurs only when manufactured or mixed gas is used. Natural gas and liquefied petroleum gas are almost always practically free from poison-ous constituents and are not likely to be breathed in sufficient quantity to cause asphyxiation. The possibility of asphyxiation by the products of incomplete combustion is equally serious in households using either natural or manufactured gas, and is by no means limited to gas-burning appliances. Wherever fuel is burned this hazard may exist,

Many hazards would be avoided if gas users would more frequently seek the advice and assistance which every gas company is glad to render. Usually the company has special facilities for dealing with every difficulty likely to arise; and it has as great an interest in safe and satisfactory service as the consumers have. In particular, the gas company should be promptly notified in any case of serious trouble and should be consulted before any unusual change is made in the equipment used. No accessory made by one manufacturer for use with an appliance should be used on another appliance without the advice of the gas company.

Meters and Regulators

Flammable materials and rubbish should not be placed near the gas meter, since a fire in such material would be likely to melt the soldered seams of the meter or its connections and the flame of the escaping gas might greatly increase the extent of the fire.

The gas meter should never be tampered with or subjected to strain. It is generally one of the weakest parts of the piping system because it is usually constructed of light sheet metal and the breaking of its case will cause the escape of gas. The householder should, therefore, allow the company to install the meter where, in its judgment, it will be safe from mechanical strains, falling objects, and other harmful conditions such as excessive heat, cold, or moisture. Meters are frequently placed on shelves or other supports to take the weight off the connections. Such support should never be removed.

The installation of so-called house governors or regulators, except those installed on the inlet side of the meter by the gas company, or those supplied as a part of the regular equipment of a house-heating furnace or other appliance requiring unusually accurate control, is seldom justified for residential service. The gas company is responsible for the delivery of gas to the user at pressures suitable for the operation of all ordinary appliances, and the obligation is usually met, often with the aid of governors. When expert service is regularly employed for the care of appliances, the use of regulators will, of course, be left to the judgment of the expert.

Turning Gas On and Off

The practice of some gas users of partially closing the shut-off valve at the meter is not advisable; it rarely, if ever, saves gas and may unfavorably affect the operation of appliances already adjusted to give the most eco-nomical and satisfactory service. With adequate piping and open valves, the use of one appliance affects another scarcely at all, but if the meter valve is closed enough to affect appreciably the gas supply to one burner, the operation of another will reduce the supply available to the first, possibly to the extent of introducing a hazard from the flashing back or extinction of the flame. Even if there is only one burner on the line and it burns gas at too high a rate, the remedy is the adjustment or replacement of the burner orifice, not interference with the gas supply.

It is well, however, to know the location of the meter shut-off cock and to have a wrench handy with which to close it in case of necessity; but having once been shut off, the gas should not be turned on again by the householder. The gas company should be notified and requested to turn on the gas. This precaution is so important that in some cities even experienced gas fitters are not allowed to turn on the gas unless actually in the employ of the gas company.

Prepayment meters, once very common in the poorer sections of cities and in resort towns, are now fortunately almost nonexistent in this country. If one must be used and if the flow of gas has stopped, the householder should never put another coin into the meter until absolutely certain that there are no open burners.

Leaks

Any leakage of gas, no matter how small, may be dangerous. Although the quantity of gas escaping may appear to be insufficient to cause asphyxiation or explosion, it is never possible to be sure of this without a chemical analysis of the mixture. Hence, one should never regard an air-gas mixture as safe, and when even a slight escape of gas is noted, shut off any equipment using the gas and immediately provide as much ventilation as possible.

"Manufactured" gases all possess distinctive odors. Strong, unpleasant scents are added to all liquefied petroleum marketed for domestic use, and much of the natural gas, but not all of it, is similarly odorized. Leakage of gas is usually first detected by odor, which is noticeable when the room is first entered even though the amount of gas present is very small. However, if a person for any reason remains in a room containing gas, he soon loses to some extent the ability to judge by the odor whether or not the air is heavily charged with it. Therefore, anyone who persists in staying in the room after the gas is smelled may in a little while not suspect that he is running any risk, even at the moment when he is on the point of losing consciousness.

Even at the start it is difficult to judge from the intensity of the odor how much gas is leaking. Therefore, it is never safe to disregard the odor of gas. The very first thing to do is to ventilate the room and then search for the leak, which will usually be at a gas cock or a joint in the connecttions. If this is quickly located by odor, sound, or by applying soap solution, and it is evident that the leakage is so small as not to permeate the room, no other precaution need be taken than the temporary use of soap to stop the leak and a notification to the gas company, so that a permanent repair may be made. Tubing that is cracked or that has loose ends, even though leaking very slightly when first noticed, should be put out of use immediately.

Never search for a gas leak with a match, candle, lantern, or with the aid of any other ordinary lighting appliance. Even the switch operating an electric light may cause a spark which will ignite an explosive mixture and thus cause disastrous results. Never try to locate the point of leakage by igniting the escaping gas, for unexpected 'pockets" of explosive mixtures may exist, as between joists, beneath stairways, or close to the ceiling, and these explode without warning. It is safer to open the windows or take other precautions—in the dark, if need be—having someone outside the affected room on the watch to render assistance if necessary. Not only is there danger of explosion, but the use of a lighted match near a lead meter connection or at the soldered seams of a meter may cause a tiny unseen flame at a point of leakage, which can melt the lead or solder, causing a larger leak and eventually a serious fire.

If the odor of gas seems to permeate the room, and the actual leak cannot be located quickly, the gas may be coming into the room through the floor or walls, No time should be lost in extinguishing all flames or fire, in opening the windows, and in seeing that all persons leave the room or, if necessary, leave the house altogether. These precautions should be taken on the bare suspicion that a serious leak may be present and before any investigation of basement or adjoining rooms is undertaken.

Do not wait for a second impression or for confirmation that the odor is not increasing or is dying away. Remember that the nose loses its sensitivity in a short time in a gas-contaminated atmosphere.

If on opening a door into the basement or an adjoining room, the odor there seems stronger, it is safer not to enter. If there is no fire or flame burning in the room, and if it is unoccupied, it is safer to close the door and leave the premises, if necessary, to wait until someone from the company arrives. If the basement or room must be entered to extinguish lights or to rescue persons sleeping or unconscious, no light should be carried except an electric flashlight which should be turned on and off only outside the room. A watcher should be stationed outside to summon aid in case the person who entered first should lose consciousness.

Gas sometimes travels for a con-

siderable distance; it may be found at points far removed from the real source of leakage. Gas in dangerous quantities may pass through the foundation walls of buildings, as from the street under frozen ground into the basement, or from the basement of an adjoining building, and also through partition walls and through floors, as from the basement to first floor rooms.

The hazard from gas which has traveled underground is likely to be underestimated for several reasons. The odorous constituents of the gas mixture are strongly absorbed by many soils; the familiar odor is likely to be disguised by the removal of some of its components and by the addition of others; and finally the development of the odor is likely to be so gradual as to escape notice in a familiar environment.

Even the slightest odor of gas, the source of which cannot be definitely located, should be immediately reported to the gas company.

In no other case is attention to the first indication of escaping gas so important as that of a buried reservoir containing liquefied petroleum gases. The fuel is in the dense form of a liquid under high pressure (for a gas distribution system) and can escape at an excessive rate through a very small opening. The escape of gas is likely to be the result of corrosion, and without inspection the extent of the corroded area cannot be estimated. A leaking tank must not be uncovered for inspection while under pressure because the removal of the supporting soil from corroded metal frequently results in opening relatively large areas.

The only thing to do is to notify the company supplying the fuel to remove what is already in the tank and make the necessary inspection and replacement or repair immediately. If expert service is not obtainable at once, gas should be burned from the system at a safe place rapidly enough to materially reduce both the temperature of the liquid and the pressure in the reservoir. The leak is not then likely to be enlarged until the fuel supply is exhausted, after which an inspection can be made safely.

Appliances

The installation and use of gas appliances requires care to avoid accidents, too. Refer to the section on *GAS APPLIANCES* for further information.

Gasket

Made of paper, metal, rubber, plastic or other composition material, a gasket performs a function similar to a hose washer. It is set between two parts, usually metal, to prevent leaking at the joint.

Gate Valve

The action of this valve depends upon the motion of a wedge-shaped disc or gate between the inlet and outlet pipes. Of all valves it offers the least amount of resistance to the flow of water, for the opening in the valve itself is the same diameter as the pipe with which it is used.

Gate valves offer about half the resistance to the water flow of an elbow and are recommended for use in areas where water pressure is low. However, the handyman cannot repair a gate valve once it starts to leak. The disc or gate is made of metal and is not easily replaced. The rubbing of the gate against dirt, grit or sand will wear the metal and make the valve leak.

This valve can be installed in any position. The stem or handle, however, should point upward when the valve is installed in a system which has to be drained for the winter. If the stem or handle points downward, some water will remain in the bonnet, or the section just under the handle. This water, when subject to cold weather, will freeze and expand. It may cause the upper section of the valve to crack. If it is necessary to install the valve in this position, it is

essential that the bonnet be removed when the line is drained. In this way, the water will be removed from the bonnet and the valve can be re-assembled and left without danger of splitting in freezing weather.

Generator

This term is applied to machines used for the transformation of mechanical energy into electrical energy. Generators are used in power plants to produce electricity.

More common to the handyman is the generator in the car. It is used to

recharge the car battery while the motor is in operation.

Another form of generator is found on bicycles. It is attached to the front

An automobile generator.

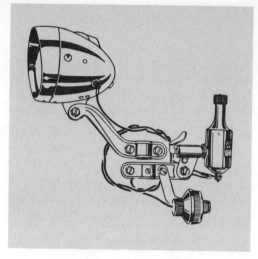

A generator used on a bicycle.

wheel of the bike and, as the wheel turns, the generator produces the current needed to light the headlight and tail light.

German Silver

This is an alloy of copper, zinc and nickel. It is used in handicraft work and also as a solder to join certain metals together.

Gimlet

This small wood-boring tool has its handle attached at right angles to the bit. It is not used frequently today.

A gimlet is used to bore small holes.

Gimp Tack

This is a small upholstery nail with a round head; it is used to tack cloth gimp to furniture.

Glass

Glass—How To Buy It

A homeowner can get a lot for his money or a little when he buys glass for windows, doors or partitions. But if he knows which glass will do what, and how to buy it, he won't pay double or triple prices for plate glass when he could have used heavy sheet glass, nor will he waste money by ordering glass by the sheet when he could have used a case.

Window glass, also called *sheet glass,* is the most commonly used in the house. In fact before glass walls and picture windows were used it was usually the only kind. It comes in two thicknesses, single strength and double strength; and in two qualities, A and B.

Grades A and B differ only in the number of small defects and waves. However, the difference is not ordinarily noticeable, and many dealers don't even stock A quality because they do not believe that it is worth a 25% premium.

Whether to use single or double strength depends mainly on window size. A good rule to follow is to use double strength for anything over about two feet square. How large can double strength glass be? If winds don't exceed 70 m.p.h., double strength glass may be used in sizes up to 38"x48", or 34"x72".

The next price jump to crystal sheet or plate glass is very sharp. If you want a window wall consider the possibilities of working it out using the indicated dimensions of double strength instead of plate glass. This can be most attractive and at about

Economical way to buy window glass is by the case. This way it is much cheaper and easier to handle. Except in very large sizes, a case contains approximately 50 square feet—for example, eight 24"x 36" sheets.

one-fourth the cost. Go right across the room with 30"x72" double-strength glass placed vertically. The distance of approximately 30" to the floor can be plain wall or used for built-in bookcases, cabinets or ventilating louvers.

Case Lots

Buying window glass by the case is one way to save money. Glass by the case doesn't cost much more than half as much as by the sheet. It's also

Plate glass top finishes this table handsomely. To order glass for rectangular one, dimensions are enough. An irregular shape should be traced on sheet of stiff paper.

Inside, looking out—Note the frost-free double glass window at left with pair of ordinary plate glass units. Inset shows the sealed air space that is built into doubleglazed units, providing valuable heat insulation and preventing condensation.

easier to handle. At economical prices you can afford to use glass liberally in anything you build or remodel or enclose. And, buying by the case does not mean you're stockpiling it for years to come. Usually a case of window glass is whatever number of sheets comes nearest to totaling 50 square feet. Cases of very large sheets contain 100 square feet.

Crystal sheet, which is heavy window glass of good quality, is the economical thing to buy when the opening is too big for double strength.

Plate glass, which is polished to optical perfection, may be ⅛″ thick or for a big view window, ¼″ thick. If you have a long-distance view through your window, you will need plate glass. Otherwise you can use crystal sheet; for short distances you will never notice the slight waviness.

For plate and usually crystal sheet, in sizes too big for you to handle and too expensive for you to risk breaking, you must figure on paying a

Heat-absorbing plate glass makes windbreak for terrace of seashore home. Panes of this type, slightly tinted, filter out sun's infrared rays.

higher installed price, which includes an expensive labor cost.

Heat-absorbing plate glass, while no substitute for air conditioning, does screen out approximately 29% of the sun's heat. It is used in west windows of seaside homes, as well as in car windows. It costs about 2½ times as much as regular plate glass.

Obscure glass is used where you want light but no visibility. For example, a wall of it might be just the

Use patterned glass wherever light without transparency is desired. There are many patterns; wide and narrow corrugations, stipples, ribs and diamond designs.

thing for a basement recreation room where part of the basement is used as a garage or workshop. For this you would need the thick kind, say ⅜". Thinner figured glass serves for entrance panels, cupboard doors and shower enclosures.

Transparent mirror glass is often used for one-way vision in entrance doors. Ready-made it is extremely expensive, but a glass dealer who makes mirrors can usually prepare it for you at about half the price.

Insulating glass is the modern, superior replacement for ordinary windows plus storm sash. Like any insulation, it usually pays for itself over the years in fuel savings as well as comfort. It consists of two or three panes sealed in units, with air spaces between the panes. A typical double glazed unit has two sheets of ¼" plate glass with a ½" air space between. Originally all insulating units were made of plate glass, but it is now made in window glass as well. Unless you need large windowpanes, you can save about one-third by using the window glass kind.

Glass Blocks

Glass blocks make an attractive entrance to a contemporary designed home.

Photograph courtesy of Pittsburgh Corning Corp.

In the long list of building materials, glass blocks rank as one of the most versatile. They can be used for exterior as well as interior walls or for partition walls that do not go entirely to the ceiling.

Glass blocks provide light plus privacy. They come in many sizes and shapes and there are special blocks made to control the sun. Furthermore, glass blocks are easy to maintain and special units are available to provide ventilation through glass block walls.

Glass blocks can be installed within a wooden frame or in a bed of mortar. Once you understand how to set glass blocks in mortar—a project you might want to undertake to replace an existing basement window with glass blocks—then you will be able to handle glass blocks within a frame inside the house. Literature on interior framing of glass blocks is readily available from glass block manufacturers.

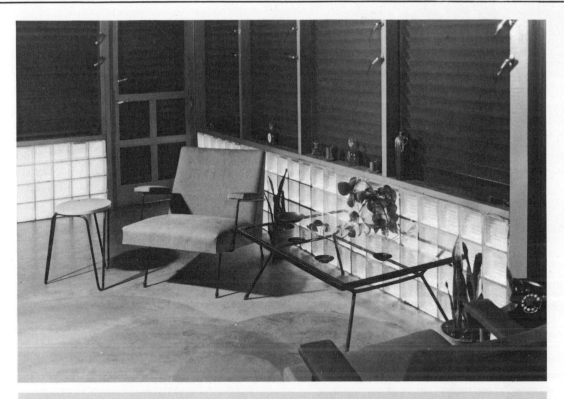

Glass blocks are an ideal way of enclosing the lower half of a porch with louver windows used above. Exterior lighting illuminates the porch at night as the light shines through the glass.

Light and privacy are assured in this glass block wall bathroom. A window is set into the glass block wall for ventilation.

It's possible to get more light in the kichen by adding a glass block wall above the kitchen sink work area.

Here glass blocks are used to add wall space between the two rooms. The large archway is made narrower by adding translucent walls.

Photograph courtesy of Pittsburgh Corning Corp.

How To Work with Glass Block

The proper mortar materials and mix are important whether for laying bricks or glass blocks.

The proper mortar materials are Portland cement, hydrated lime, sand, water, and waterproofing compound. The addition of an integral waterproofer of the water-repellent type is an added measure to insure watertight joints. Manufacturer's specifications concerning the use of this material should be followed very closely. Where a waterproof masonry mortar is used, no additional waterproofer should be added to the mix. For better results, accelerators and antifreeze compounds should not be used.

ACCURATE MEASUREMENT

The accurate measurement of materials is important. Generally a 1–1–4 mortar mix is satisfactory. However, reasonable variations from the mix are permitted and allowable limits are covered by manufacturer's specifications.

MORTAR CONSISTENCY

The consistency of the mortar mix has a direct bearing on the strength and weather-proofness of the joints. Since glass blocks have no suction like bricks, the mortar must be drier . . . it should not flow or have too much slump. Too wet a mix makes it extremely difficult to get proper alignment of block joints, and cleaning time is greatly increased. The mix should be not too dry, not too wet, but just right. Here is a good thing to remember: Do not re-temper mortar after the initial set has taken place.

1. The sill is cleaned of dirt or foreign materials. The next step in preparing the opening to receive glass blocks is the application of a heavy coat of asphalt emulsion to the sill . . . only to the area to be covered by the mortar bed joint. The emulsion must be dry before the mortar is applied. This generally takes two hours.

2. Check the dimensions of the opening, then mark off the spacing for the courses of block at the jambs and sill. Glass block sizes are modular. This modular coordination with other building materials makes it easy for the mason to lay out his work. Proper marking of courses eliminates any need for fudging joint thickness in the last courses laid. Where practical, story poles can be used for joint spacing.

3. For panels of glass block over 25 square feet in area, expansion spaces are required at the side jambs and heads of the openings. To prevent mortar bridging the expansion space, strips of expansion joint material are placed at these points and held by gobs of asphalt emulsion on the back of the strip. The first strip must be placed tight against the sill, and as the panel goes up, additional strips are placed. If desired, these strips can be applied for the entire panel prior to the blocks being laid. The expansion strips are 4⅛" wide, 25" long and ⅜" thick.

4. The careful preparations show dividends as you set the first block in place on the mortar bed joint. After the block has been set, pieces of cardboard cut from the glass block carton dividers are placed between the sides of the block and the chase. Wood wedges are sometimes used for this purpose, but by using cardboard, excess mortar which would have to be removed later, cannot get into the chase.

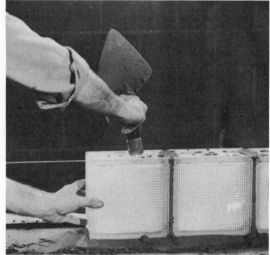

5. To insure plumb and level work, work to a guide line. A block is set in the middle of long panels to prevent line sag.

The accurate squareness and thickness of all glass blocks helps you get a plumb level job with good joint alignment.

Note rubber crutch tip on the mason's trowel. This avoids any possibility of chipping the glass when the mason taps the block to get alignment of joints.

6. To insure weather-tight joints all bed and head joints should be full of mortar. Full joints can be obtained by slightly crowning the mortar.

To get a full joint at the corners of the blocks, the mortar should be cut off square at the ends . . . as it is placed on the block. The heavy application of grit on the mortar bond coating prevents slippage of the mortar from the block.

7. When you furrow the bed and head joint mortar, voids are caused. Driving rail often forces itself into these voids. These voids or channels in the mortar joints provide an easy passage for any water which has penetrated through cracks at the face of the joint. The final result is a leaking panel. Remember, don't furrow mortar joints.

We all know that a full mortar joint is necessary to keep water out. Here is what happens if you furrow the bed and head joint mortar. The block in this picture has been removed from the panel. See the void caused by furrowing . . . it will provide an easy passage for water.

8. Properly crowned mortar joints are shown in photograph 6. With the mortar slightly crowned, a full joint will be obtained without voids. This will result in a water-tight panel.

Here is what happens when the head joint mortar is not furrowed.

Look at the mortar on the edge of this block taken from the panel. The full impression of the key-lock edge profile on this block shows that the joint was full.

9. Wall ties are placed in horizontal joints of the panel according to building code requirements. Generally, the spacing is every 24″ regardless of block size.

Wall ties . . . 1) should be used immediately below and above openings in panels . . . 2) Should not bridge expansion spaces . . . 3) Should lap minimum of 6″ when more than a single length is used . . . 4) Should not touch glass. To avoid this . . . lay half bed joint . . . press wall tie in place . . . complete bed joint. Wall ties are welded galvanized wire mesh 8′ long, 2″ wide with cross wires spaced every 8″.

10. Where ventilators are installed, many methods or windows can be used. Here all the blocks in the first course at the vent have been laid with an opening left for the vent. The vent is then placed in position on a mortar bed, plumbed and levelled.

As these units are generally small, no expansion space is required and mortar is tamped solidly between the vent and blocks. Wall ties are used in the joints at the sill and the head of the ventilators.

11. The panel is now ready for the last block. First install the block at the jamb, then butter the block edges of the opening. The last block is buttered, tilted up and shoved into place. The joints are then pointed so that no voids will occur.

12. Final appearance and weather-tightness depend on the care with which you tool the joints. The joints should be concave and smooth to provide best protection against water penetration. Pressure on the tool reveals joints which are not full; these joints should be tuck pointed as tooling progresses.

13. Cleaning should be done before the mortar reaches its final set. If proper mix and amount of mortar are used, cleaning will be simple: fiber brush to remove excess mortar, a rag to clean the surfaces.

14. The final result of care in selection and preparation of materials, and of good masonry workmanship is strong weathertight joints.

Note the smooth concave mortar joints which reveal the block edges as sharp, clean lines.

15. Free movement of the panel with support against wind loads is provided by tightly packed oakum between the chase and panel. A space should be left for calking.

16. The final step in the installation is the calking of the panel perimeter. When this is done, the panel will withstand satisfactorily the weather and wind loads to which it will be exposed over the lifetime of the building.

Photographs courtesy of Pittsburgh Corning Corporation.

PANELS OF GLASS BLOCK 35 SQ. FT. OR LESS

In this type of construction the maximum area is 35 square feet with maximum width 5′ and height 7′. The general practice is to use an expansion space at the side jambs of all glass block panels. However, for small panels as illustrated here the blocks can be mortared in solid at the side jambs. It is necessary, however, to keep a finger space between brick withes about ¾″ deep. This allows the mortar to key in at jamb and secure panel.

Glass block panels, regardless of area or size, are nonload bearing and require space at the head to take care of expansion and lintel deflection.

PANELS OF GLASS BLOCK BETWEEN 25 AND 100 SQ. FT.

Where it is desirable to show the full face of the block panel, chases cannot be used for lateral support. Proper support can be obtained by using wall anchors if the area is not over 100 square feet and neither panel dimension is over 10′. The wall anchors should be spaced 24″ apart —and occur in the same joint as the wall tie. To permit free movement of the panel, the anchors are crimped or bent in the expansion space. As a space for calking must be provided, a standard expansion strip is easily cut to 3″ width to be inserted between the anchors with gobs of asphalt emulsion. Local code authorities in some areas may restrict the use of wall anchor construction.

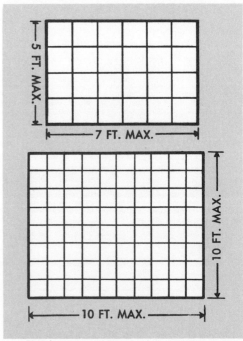

Sketch courtesy of Pittsburgh Corning Corporation.

Glass Cutter

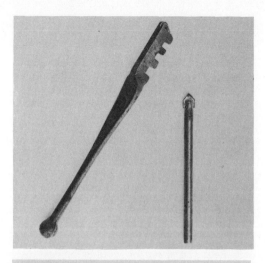

On the left is a glass cutter most frequently used by the handyman. On the right is a glass drilling bit to make holes in glass.

This tool is used to cut glass to size. Usually, a glass cutter has a small rotary wheel or diamond set in the handle.

There are also glass cutting bits for drilling holes in glass. These special bits require the use of a lubricant while cutting. It is best to make a 'well' or 'dish' around the spot to be drilled by using putty to form the walls. Then pour a little turpentine or oil into the 'dish' to lubricate the bit while it is cutting through the glass.

Glass Cutting

While you can usually buy glass cut to size, there are times when it is necessary to cut the glass yourself. When you watch an expert cut glass, it looks easy enough. Well, here's how to cut glass like an expert.

All you need is a quality glass cutter, a straightedge and some lubricating oil.

It is essential that the glass be perfectly clean. Wipe the surface off with a clean cloth for any dirt or a film over the glass will prevent the glass cutter from making a uniform cut. Now follow the simple step-by-step procedure.

1. Lubricate the wheel of your glass cutter using any household oil, such as 3-in-One. This lubricating of the wheel reduces friction between the glass and the edge of the wheel.

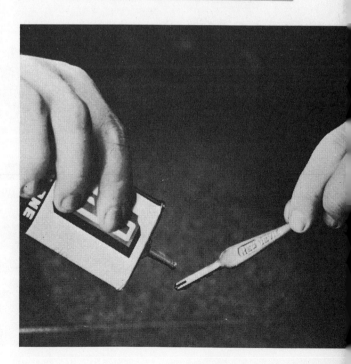

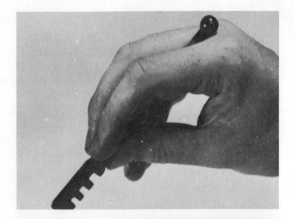

2. Here's how to hold the glass cutter correctly. The right way is between the first and second fingers with your thumb on the under side of the handle. Do not squeeze too hard.

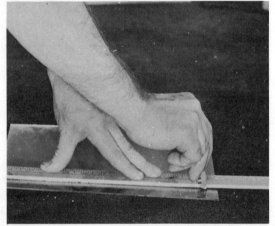

3. Rest the glass on several sheets of newspaper or a piece of felt. If you use a yardstick as a straight edge, moisten the bottom so that it won't slip on the glass. Gently, but firmly, press the cutter to the glass, holding it upright. Start about ⅛″ from the edge farthest from you. Make a straight, even and continuous stroke across the whole surface and off the very edge of the glass.

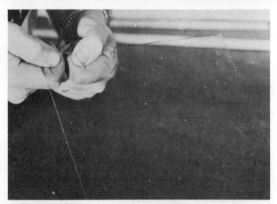

4. To break the glass, hold it firmly on opposite sides of the cut line. Then give a quick bending motion away from the cut. Keep your fingers and thumbs as close to the cut line as possible. Be careful . . . hold firmly. Always break right after cutting so that the cut does not get "cold."

5. Here's what not to do! This shows how hesitation during cutting stroke leaves an uneven spot. This causes the break to curve from the straight line. An even, firm, positive cutting stroke avoids this result.

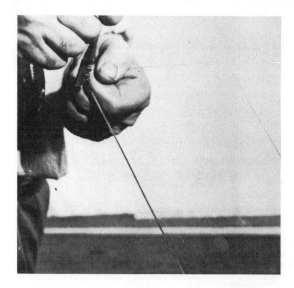

6. The slots in the end of the glass cutter are used for breaking off narrow strips. If you have to break off a narrow strip, hold the glass in one hand and the cutter in the other. A firm movement will separate the glass at the cut. Tapping the underside of the glass, immediately after making the cut, may make the glass separate more easily.

Fancy Glass Cutting

Once you have learned how to cut a straight line, you might feel adventurous and try some fancy glass cutting. Free-form lines and circles are not too difficult if you have the proper tools and knowledge. There are available circle cutters for glass which will cut circles from 2″ to 24″ in diameter.

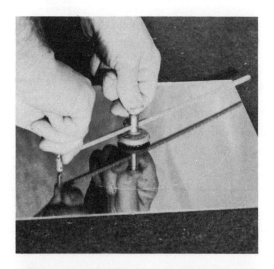

1. A circle cutter is used in the same manner as a regular cutter. Set the glass on a proper base and place the rubber suction cup in the exact center of the circle. Swing the cutter around but do not overlap at the end of the circle. Hold the glass in your hands and press with your fingers to impress the circle right after cutting so that the etched line won't get "cold."

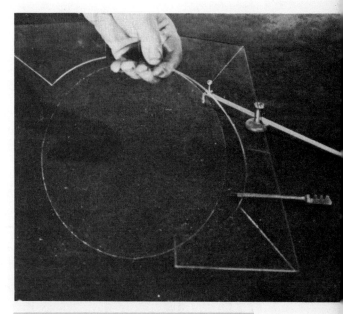

2. The glass surrounding the circle must be cut with a regular cutter to free the circle. Make several straight cuts from the circle to the edge of the glass and then break away the circle.

Photographs courtesy of Red Devil Tools.

Glass Tinting

It is possible to achieve artistic effects on ordinary glass which almost resemble the ancient art of stained glass.

Many good art supply stores, or art supply departments in department stores, carry these glass paints in stock. They are especially formulated for the purpose, being translucent rather than opaque.

A wide range of colors is to be found in this unusual product, many of them having warm, jewel-like tones which glow beautifully when light is passed through them.

Full instructions for their use is found on the packages.

Glazier's Chisel

This is a wide but thin chisel. It is used for removal of window trim and molding.

Because of the thin blade, it is usually possible to remove the trim or molding with this chisel without any appreciable damage to the painted surface.

It can also be used for removal of the shoe mold of the baseboard or even crown molding along the ceiling without marring the surfaces.

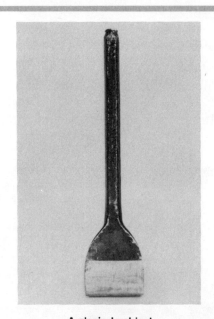

A glazier's chisel.

Glazier's Points

These are small, flat, triangular metal pieces which are used in addition to putty to hold the glass window pane in place. For information on the way they are used, see the section on *GLAZING—WINDOWS*.

Glazing— Windows

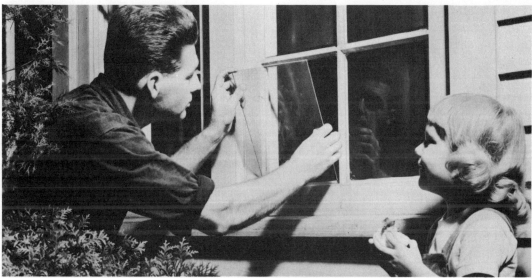

Photograph courtesy of Libbey-Owens-Ford Glass Co.

A broken windowpane can be replaced without much difficulty. It is usually advisable to remove the sash which contains the broken pane, especially an upstairs window, and lay it on a flat surface such as table or workbench, although if the window is on the ground floor, the pane may be replaced with the aid of a stepladder.

Materials Needed

You will need: chisel or jackknife for removing putty and for driving in glazier's points; putty knife; rule to measure size of glass needed; small flat paint brush; glass cutter (if you intend to cut glass); yardstick or steel square; glass of the same thickness as the broken pane; glazier's points; putty; raw linseed oil to soften the putty and be used as a primer; and matching paint for the putty after it has hardened. Good putty suitable for ordinary household use can be made by mixing the best grade of whiting and pure raw linseed oil, or may be obtained already mixed from hardware and paint dealers.

Removing Old Glass and Putty

Broken glass should be removed from the sash and the old putty chipped off with a chisel or jackknife. Glazier's points should be pulled, and the wood where the new glass is to rest should be scraped well with an old jackknife or similar tool. The wood should then be given a coat of thin paint or linseed oil to act as a primer and prevent the oil in the putty from being absorbed by the wood and the putty from drying out and crumbling.

Measuring for New Glass

Measure accurately the size of the needed glass and give the dimensions to the hardware or paint dealer, letting him cut the pane to the proper size, if you prefer not to cut the glass at home. All four sides from wood to wood in the sash should be measured and 1/8″ to 3/16″ deducted to allow for expansion and irregularities. Measuring the four sides is advisable because some sashes are not true and do not form a perfect rectangle. Most of the window glass stocked by dealers is designated as "double strength clear American."

Setting Glass

A thin coat of putty, about 1/16″ thick, should be spread on the rabbet or groove in the sash for the glass to rest in, and the pane placed in the sash. Care should be taken to have the putty evenly distributed so that unfilled gaps will not appear between the sash and the glass. By pressing gently on the glass to imbed the edges of the pane in the putty, the pane can be made watertight and the cushion of putty thus formed will reduce the possibility of cracking the glass when glazier's points are put in.

1. To protect your hands, wear gloves when removing the broken pieces of glass. This is best done from the putty side.

2. Use an old chisel to remove any old putty. If it's hard, you can use a soldering iron to soften the putty or else tap the chisel lightly with a hammer, or preferably with a mallet.

3. Use a rule or a steel tape to measure rather than a cloth tape. Measure the exact height and width of the opening on the outside of the sash.

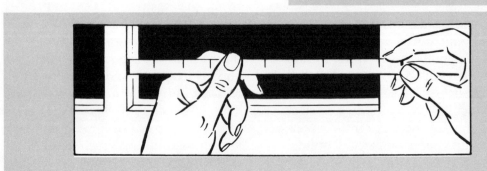

Glazier's points are small, flat, triangular metal pieces used in addition to putty to hold the glass in place. They should be laid on the glass, about three or four to a side, on the long sides first, and forced into the sash with the side edge of a chisel or screw driver by sliding the tool over the surface of the glass. If the glass is still loose after the points have been set, remove those which do not fit well and replace them, pressing the glass more firmly against the bed of putty during the process.

Use of Putty

Putty is usually purchased in a can with a lid which provides an airtight seal. To prepare the putty for use, it should be kneaded on a nonabsorptive surface such as a glass plate until the mass is pliable. Putty that remains in the can after use may be kept for some time by pouring a thin film of linseed oil over it to keep it pliable and by placing waxed paper or foil immediately on top of the oil

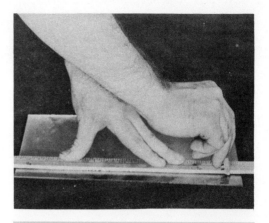

4. Buy the glass cut to size or cut it yourself. It's best if the pane of glass is ⅛" to 3/16" smaller than the vertical and horizontal measurements of the window.

as a seal. Upon removing the waxed paper or foil, and kneading the putty, it will again be ready for use.

For application to the sash, a small piece of putty should be rolled out between the palms of the hands to form a pencil-shaped roll. The rolls should then be laid end to end on the glass where it abuts the sash, one side at a time. The putty should be

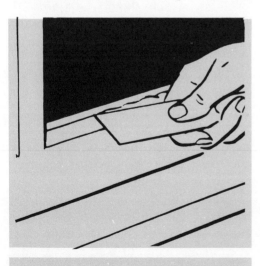

5. Before inserting the new glass, apply a thin layer of putty in the rabbet of the sash where the glass will rest. Apply with a putty knife.

6. Lay the glass in putty bed and press against sash. Then drive or press glazier's points into wood. Use three or four to a side, starting with a long side.

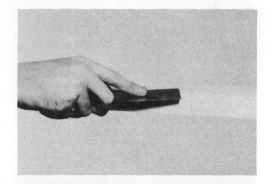

7. After points have been applied, roll some putty in your hands and press another layer on over the glass and the sash, doing one side at a time. Smooth with putty knife.

Photograph courtesy of Red Devil Tools.

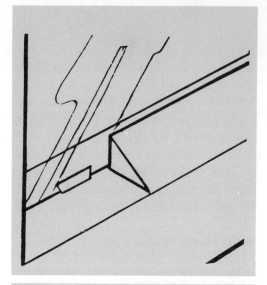

8. This is the way the smoothed putty should look against the window pane. A portion has been removed in this sketch so that you get a cross-sectional view. Finally, paint the surface.

Sketches courtesy of Libbey-Owens-Ford Glass Co.

pressed down firmly but gently with a putty knife, drawing it along the sash from one end to the other. To lessen the danger of breaking the glass by strong pressure, the putty should be soft and pliable. The putty knife should be held at an angle, guided by the glass and sash, to form a smooth bevel. Excess putty spreading beyond this bevel should be cut off and used to fill any depressions that have occurred. Care should be taken not to spread the putty far enough over the surface to show on the inside of the window. The same procedure should be followed for the other sides of the sash.

Putty stains may be removed from the glass with a cloth moistened with turpentine or gasoline. After a day or two, when the putty has hardened, it should be painted to match the window sash.

Metal Sash

Most metal sash are constructed so that the glass may be replaced with little difficulty. There are many kinds of metal sash, however, and the steps to be taken may vary to some extent. The manufacturer usually issues instructions for using his particular product, which should be followed. In case of an emergency, where no such information is at hand, one of the following methods may be used:

The tools and materials needed are screw driver, putty knife, and small flat paint brush; doublestrength glass or plate glass; putty made of whiting and white lead; and enough paint of the same color the sash for covering the top coat of putty.

Some windows are glazed on the outside, while others are glazed on the inside of the sash. In either case, the old putty and broken glass should be removed and the metal sash scraped clean where the new glass is to rest. If wire spring clips were used to hold the glass, they will have to be removed before the glass can be taken out. The new glass should then be imbedded in putty to prevent it from being in direct contact with the metal. The putty should be spread over the metal where the glass is to rest and the glass pushed firmly into place so that putty fills every crevice. The glass can then be fastened tightly with wire spring clips, placed in the holes which have already been bored through the sash. When the glass is thus firmly secured, putty may be applied in the same manner as for wooden sash. After the putty has thoroughly hardened, it should be painted the same color as the sash.

In some other types of metal windows, the broken glass may be taken out by unscrewing and removing the metal beading or glazing strips and scraping the old bedding putty from the sash. The new glass can then be imbedded in putty, as described in the foregoing. When it has been placed, the metal beading or glazing strips should be refastened tightly against it. These strips will form a neat frame around the glass, which is usually held in place by brass screws.

Also see *GLASS CUTTING*.

Glides, Casters and Rests

Glides are metal, plastic, or rubber plates, discs or cushions used under the legs of furniture to protect the floor. They are needed to prevent indentations in resilent flooring materials, scratching, staining and sometimes indentation of wooden floors and the flattening of carpets and rugs.

Casters are wheel or ball-bearing units used to make furniture easily movable. They are attached to the bottom of the leg in place of a glide.

Rests serve the same function as glides but are not attached to the furniture. They are placed under the furniture leg between it and the floor.

Adjustable casters and glides have been gaining in popularity because it has been realized that many of our furniture faults—sticky drawers, doors that refuse to stay closed, etc. —are caused by uneven settling of the furniture on uneven floors.

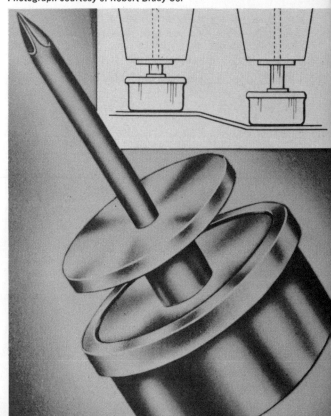

Photograph courtesy of Robert Brady Co.

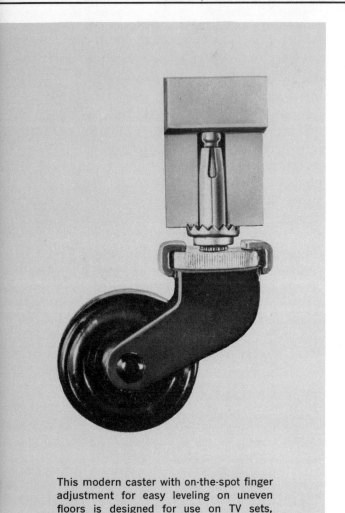

This modern caster with on-the-spot finger adjustment for easy leveling on uneven floors is designed for use on TV sets, washing machines and other furnishings.

cause is uneven floor condition.

Why are there so many uneven floors? The answer is that even the best floors will wear unevenly or settle unevenly. What makes floors settle and become uneven? Underground water, leaky water mains, weathering of building materials, traffic vibrations, earth tremors all have a part in creating uneven floors. Articles placed on such floors either wobble or settle.

Wobbling jars mechanisms of motorized equipment. Appliances, TV sets and phonographs serve better without this jarring,

When furniture settles on uneven floors, their frames are twisted out of line. This causes doors and drawers

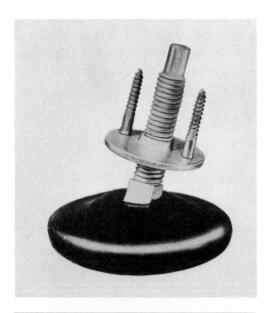

This tiltable base glide is designed for use on heavy pieces where slope or worn spots on uneven floors would cause one edge of the glide to dig into the floor covering. Tiltable feature prevents bends of the stem by assuring broad supporting surface on glide base regardless of floor.

Photograph courtesy of Adjustable Caster Co.

The symptoms of uneven floor troubles are an everyday experience to most people. Without stretching one's memory, we can vividly recall the wobbly restaurant table with a wad of paper or matchbook shoved under a leg, a wobble-dancing washing machine, a sticky door or drawer, that wobbly TV set partly on and off the rug. All of these are in need of controlled support, and we probably blame the manufacturer for making faulty furniture when the underlying

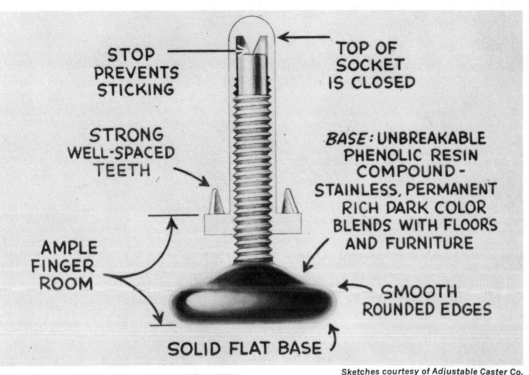

STOP PREVENTS STICKING

TOP OF SOCKET IS CLOSED

STRONG WELL-SPACED TEETH

BASE: UNBREAKABLE PHENOLIC RESIN COMPOUND - STAINLESS, PERMANENT RICH DARK COLOR BLENDS WITH FLOORS AND FURNITURE

AMPLE FINGER ROOM

SMOOTH ROUNDED EDGES

SOLID FLAT BASE

Sketches courtesy of Adjustable Caster Co.

How an adjustable glide as well as caster works: threaded section inside outside sleeve allows finger-tip adjustment.

Here are several types of glides and rests. The one in the upper left is designed for use with metal tubular furniture. After it is inserted into the tube, the parachute washer expands and prevents it from coming loose. On the right (top and bottom) are rests for round and square legs.

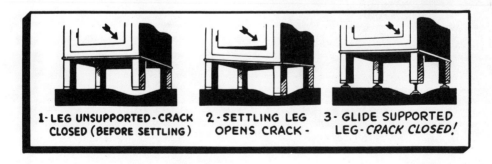

1 - LEG UNSUPPORTED - CRACK CLOSED (BEFORE SETTLING)

2 - SETTLING LEG OPENS CRACK -

3 - GLIDE SUPPORTED LEG - *CRACK CLOSED!*

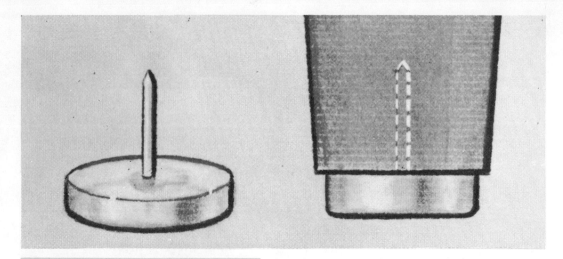

Clear plastic is sometimes used for glides. The button type with a nail in the center is hammered into the chair leg.

to rub. If they rub hard enough, they stick and cannot be closed or locked. Unclosed furniture doors and drawers invite dust.

Furniture is frequently moved around in the home so that it is subjected to settling anew each time it is moved. These frequent settlings over a period of time result in loos-

ened glue joints.

It is plain that a modern caster and glide with controlled support helps to protect furniture and equipment placed on uneven floors. The old concept of protecting floors from furniture legs is now supplemented by the important idea of protecting valuable pieces from uneven floors.

Another way to protect floors from metal tubular furniture is with special glides or crutch tips, which fit over the metal.

Photograph courtesy of Plastiglide Mfg. Corp.

Globe Valve

A globe valve resembles the standard kitchen faucet in operation. It is closed by forcing a washer down upon the valve seat by turning a handle.

Globe valves are made with a composition washer or a metal disc. The latter is used for hot water and steam lines. A globe valve with a composition washer is easily repaired, but the type with a metal disc is not.

When installing a globe valve, you should set it on the pipe so that the flow of the water is up through the orifice or opening and the washer is moved against the flow of the water when closing.

The globe valve is used widely in household plumbing despite the fact that it markedly reduces the flow of water through the pipes. Its main advantage is the fact that it is easy to change washers in this type of valve. A globe valve offers about eight times more resistance than an ordinary pipe elbow and about 16 times more resistance to the flow of water than a gate valve.

Also see *VALVES*.

A globe valve is commonly used in household plumbing. It should be installed so that the inlet pipe allows water to flow through the orifice and up.

Gouge

This is a special wood-cutting chisel with either a concave or convex cutting edge, that is, with the bevel ground either inside or outside the curved edge. Gouges are used not only in general woodworking, but also in wood turning and wood carving.

Glossary of Building and Wood-working Terms

The building trades have a special vocabulary all their own; in ordering materials and reading plans or blueprints, these terms will be of use to you:

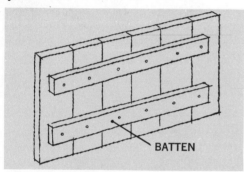

BATTEN

Anchor—Irons of special form used to fasten together timbers or masonry.

Backing—The bevel on the top edge of a hip rafter that allows the roofing boards to fit the top of the rafter without leaving a triangular space between it and the lower side of the roof covering.

Balloon frame—The lightest and most economical form of construction, in which the studding and corner posts are set up in continuous lengths from first-floor line or sill to the roof plate.

Baluster—A small column used to support a rail.

Balustrade—A row of balusters with the rails, generally used for porches, balconies, etc.

Band—A low, flat molding.

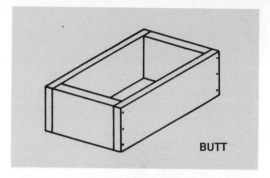

BUTT

Base—The bottom of a column; the finish of a room at the junction of the walls and floor.

Batten (cleat)—A narrow strip of board used to fasten several pieces together.

Batter board—A temporary framework used to assist in locating the corners when laying out a foundation.

Beam—An inclusive term for joists, girders, rafters, and purlins.

Bedding—A filling of mortar, putty, or other substance in order to secure a firm bearing.

Belt course—A horizontal board across or around a building, usually made of a flat member and a molding.

Bevel board (pitch board)—A board used in framing a roof or stairway to lay out bevels.

Board—Lumber less than 2 inches thick.

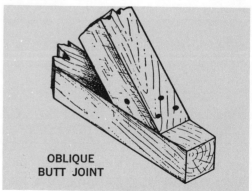

OBLIQUE BUTT JOINT

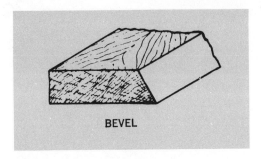

BEVEL

Board foot—The equivalent of a board 1 foot square and 1 inch thick.

Boarding in—The process of nailing boards on the outside studding of a house.

Braces—Pieces fitted and firmly fastened to two others at any angle in order to strengthen the angle thus treated.

Bracket—A projecting support for a shelf or other structure.

Break joints—To arrange joints so that they do not come directly under or over the joints of adjoing pieces, as in shingling, siding, etc.

Bridging—Pieces fitted in pairs from the bottom of one floor joist to the top of adjacent joists, and crossed to distribute the floor load; sometimes pieces of width equal to the joist and fitted neatly between them.

Building paper—Cheap, thick paper, used to insulate a building before the siding or roofing is put on; sometimes placed between double floors.

Built-up timber—A timber made of several pieces fastened together and forming one of larger dimension.

Carriages—The supports of the steps and risers of a flight of stairs.

Casement—A window in which the sash opens upon hinges.

Casing—The trimming around a door or window opening, either outside or inside, or the finished lumber around a post or beam, etc.

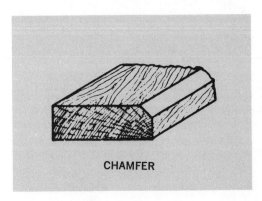

CHAMFER

Ceiling—Narrow, matched boards; sheathing of the surfaces that inclose the upper side of a room.

Center-hung sash—A sash hung on its centers so that it swings on a horizontal axis.

Chamfer—A beveled surface cut upon the corner of a piece of wood.

Checks—Split or cracks in a board, ordinarily caused by seasoning.

Clamp—A mechanical device used to hold two or more pieces together.

Clapboards—A special form of outside covering of a house; siding.

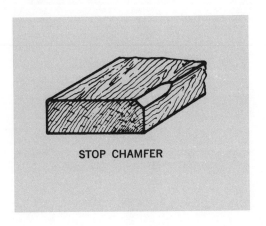

STOP CHAMFER

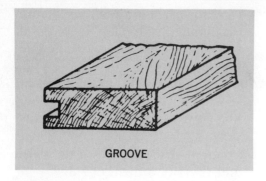

GROOVE

Columns—A support, square, rectangular, or cylindrical in section, for roofs, ceilings, etc., composed of base, shaft, and capital.

Combination frame—A combination of the principal features of the full and balloon frames.

Concrete—A combination of sand, broken stone, or gravel, and cement used in foundations, building construction for walks, etc.

Conductors—Pipes for conducting water from a roof to the ground or to a receptacle or drain; downspout.

Cornice—The molded projection which finishes the top of the wall of a building.

Counterflashings—Strips of metal used to prevent water from entering the top edge of the vertical side of a roof flashing; they also allow expansion and contraction without danger of breaking the flashing.

Deadening — Construction intended to prevent the passage of sound.

Drip—The projection of a window sill or water table to allow the water to drain clear of the side of the house below it.

Fascia—A flat member of a cornice or other finish, generally the board of the cornice to which the gutter is fastened.

Flashing—The material used and the process of making watertight the roof intersections and other exposed places on the outside of the house.

Flue—The opening in a chimney through which smoke passes.

Flush—Adjacent surfaces even, or in same plane (with reference to two structural pieces).

Footing courses—The bottom and heaviest courses of a piece of masonry.

Foundation—That part of a building or wall which supports the superstructure.

Frame—The surrounding or inclosing woodwork of windows, doors, etc., and the timber skeleton of a building.

Framing—The rough timber structure of a building, including interior and exterior walls, floor, roof, and ceilings.

Full frame—The old-fashioned mortised-and-tenoned frame, in which every joint was mortised and tenoned. Rarely used at the present time.

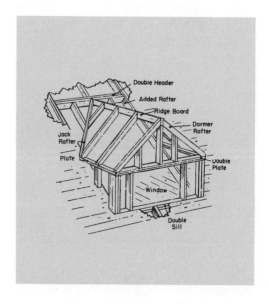

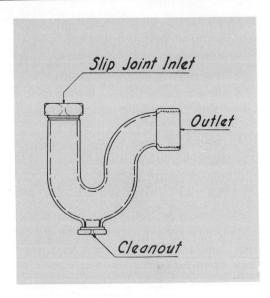

Slip Joint Inlet

Outlet

Cleanout

Furring—Narrow strips of board nailed upon the walls and ceilings to form a straight surface upon which to lay the laths or other finish.

Gable—The vertical triangular end of a building from the eaves to the apex of the roof.

Gage (gauge)—A tool used by carpenters; to strike a line parallel to the edge of the board.

Gambrel—A symmetrical roof with two different pitches or slopes on each side.

Girders—A timber used to support wall beams or joists.

Girt (ribband) — The horizontal member of the walls of a full or combination frame house which supports the floor joists or is flush with the top of the joists.

Groove—A long hollow channel cut by a tool, into which a piece fits or in which it works. Carpenters have given special names to certain forms of grooves, such as dadoes and housings. A *dado* is a rectangular groove cut across the grain the full width of the piece.

Dadoes are used in sliding doors, window frames, etc. A *housing* is a groove cut at any angle with the grain and partway across the piece. Housings are used for framing stair risers and treads into a string (not stringer). Grooving is used largely in the fastening of boards together or in the prevention of warping and twisting of wide boards or boards glued together. In doing this it is necessary to prevent the warping but to permit the free swelling and shrinking due to changes in the humidity. Various simple devices are used, such as hardwood batten, tapering key, or iron rod. Grooving is required in the first two.

Ground—A strip of wood assisting the plasterer in making a straight wall and in giving a place to which the finish of the room may be nailed.

Ground floor—The floor of a building on a level with the ground or nearly so.

Header—A short joist supporting tail beams and framed between trimmer joists; the piece of stud or finish over an opening; a lintel.

Headroom—The clear space between floor line and ceiling, as in a stairway.

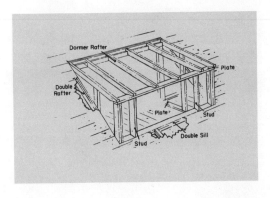

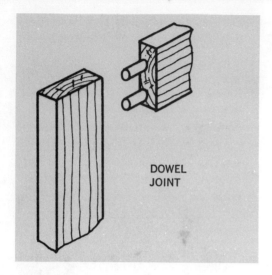

DOWEL JOINT

Heel of a rafter—The end or foot that rests on the wall plate.

Hip roof—A roof which slopes up toward the center from all sides, necessitating a hip rafter at each corner.

Jack rafter—A short rafter framing between the wall plate and a hip rafter.

Jamb—The side piece or post of an opening; sometimes applied to the doorframe.

Joints

    Butt—Squared ends or ends and edges adjoining each other.

    Dovetail—Joint made by cutting pins the shape of dovetails in which fit between dovetails upon another piece.

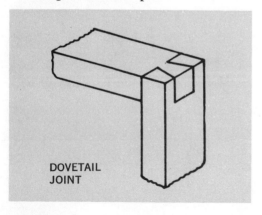

DOVETAIL JOINT

Drawboard—A mortise-and-tenon joint with holes so bored that when a pin is driven through, the joint becomes tighter.

Fished — An end butt splice strengthened by pieces nailed on the sides.

Halved—A joint made by cutting half the wood away from each piece so as to bring the sides flush.

Housed—A joint in which a piece is grooved to receive the piece which is to form the other part of the joint.

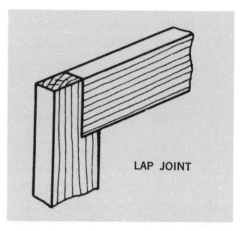

LAP JOINT

Glue—A joint held together with glue.

Lap—A joint of two pieces lapping over each other.

Mortised—A joint made by cutting a hole or mortise, in one piece, and a tenon, or piece to fit the hole, upon the other.

Rub—A flue joint made by carefully fitting the edges together, spreading glue between them, and rubbing the pieces back and forth until the pieces are well-rubbed together.

Scarfed—A timber spliced by cutting various shapes of shoulders, or jogs, which fit each other.

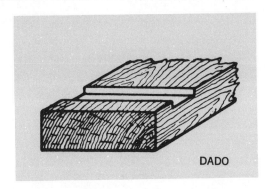

DADO

Joists—Timbers supporting the floor boards.

Kerf—The cut made by a saw.

Laths—Narrow strips to support plastering.

Lattice—Crossed wood, iron plate, or bars.

Ledgerboard—The support for the second-floor joists of a baloon-frame house, or for similar uses; ribband.

Level—A term describing the position of a line or plane when parallel to the surface of still water, an instrument or tool used in testing for horizontal and vertical surfaces, and in determining differences of elevation.

Lintel (header)—The piece of construction or finish, stone, wood or metal, which is over an opening; a header.

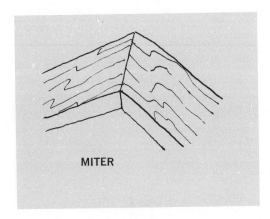

MITER

Lookout—The end of a rafter, or the construction which projects beyond the sides of a house to support the eaves; also the projecting timbers at the gables which support the verge boards.

Louver—A kind of window, generally in the peaks of gables and the tops of towers, provided with horizontal slots which exclude rain and snow and allow ventilation.

Lumber—Sawed parts of a log such as boards, planks, scantling, and timber.

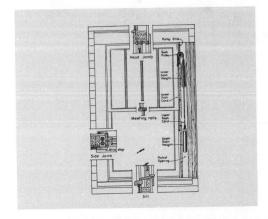

Matching, or tonguing and grooving—The method used in cutting the edges of a board to make a tongue on one edge and a groove on the other.

Meeting rail—The bottom rail of the upper sash, and the top rail of the lower sash of a double-hung window. Sometimes called the check rail.

Miter—The joint formed by two abutting pieces meeting at an angle.

Molding

　　Base—The molding on the top of a base board.

　　Bed—A molding used to cover the joint between the plancier and frieze; also used as a base molding upon heavy work, and sometimes as a member of a cornice.

Lip—A molding with a lip which overlaps the piece against which the back of the molding rests.

Rake—The cornice upon the gable edge of a pitch roof, the members of which are made to fit those of the molding of the horizontal eaves.

Picture—A molding shaped to form a support for picture hooks, often placed at some distance from the ceiling upon the wall to form the lower edge of the frieze.

Mortise—The hole which is to receive a tenon, or any hole cut into or through a piece by a chisel; generally of rectangular shape.

Mullion—The construction between the openings of a window frame to accommodate two or more windows.

Muntin—The vertical member between two panels of the same piece of panel work. The vertical sashbars separating the different panes of glass.

Newel—The principal post at the foot of a staircase; also the central support of a winding flight of stairs.

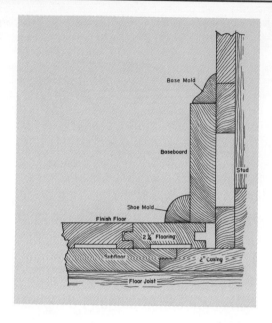

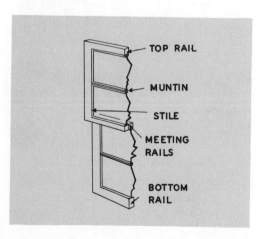

Nosing—The part of a stair tread which projects over the riser, or any similar projection; a term applied to the rounded edge of a board.

Piers—Masonry supports, set independently of the main foundation.

Pilaster—A portion of a square column, usually set within or against a wall.

Piles—Long posts driven into the soil in swampy locations or whenever it is difficult to secure a firm foundation, upon which the footing course of masonry or other timbers are laid.

Pitch—Inclination or slope, as of roofs or stairs, or the rise divided by the span.

Pitch board—A board sawed to the exact shape formed by the stair tread, riser slope of the stairs and used to lay out the carriage and stringers.

Plan—A horizontal geometrical section of a building, showing the walls, doors, windows, stairs, chimney, columns, etc.

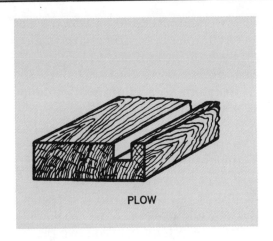

PLOW

Planks or lumber—Material 2 or 3 inches thick and more than 4 inches wide, such as joists, flooring, etc.

Plaster—A mixture of lime, hair, and sand, or of lime, cement, and sand, used to cover outside and inside wall surfaces.

Plate—The top horizontal piece of the wall of a frame building upon which the roof rests.

Plate cut—The cut in a rafter which rests upon the plate; sometimes called the seat cut.

Plumb cut—Any cut made in a vertical plane; the vertical cut at the top end of a rafter.

Ply—A term used to denote a layer or thickness of building or roofing paper as two-ply, three-ply, etc.

Porch—An ornamental entrance way.

Post—A timber set on end to support a wall, girder, or other member of the structure.

Plow—To cut a groove running in the same direction as the grain of the wood.

Pulley stile—The member of a window frame which contains the pulleys, and between which the edges of the sash slide.

Purlin—A timber supporting several rafters at one or more points, or the roof sheeting directly.

Rabbet or rebate—A corner cut out of an edge of a piece of wood.

Rafters
> **Common** — Those which run square with the plate and extend to the ridge.
>
> **Cripple**—Those which cut between valley and hip rafters.
>
> **Hip**—Those extending from the outside angle of the plates toward the apex of the roof.
>
> **Jacks**—Those square with the plate and intersecting the hip rafter.
>
> **Valley**—Those extending from an inside angle of the plates toward the ridge or center line of the house.

Rail—The horizontal members of a balustrade or panel work.

Rake—The trim of a building extending in an oblique line, as rake dado or molding.

Return—The continuation of a molding or finish of any kind in a different direction.

Ribband—(See *Ledgerboard*.)

Ridge—The top edge or corner formed by the intersection of two roof surfaces.

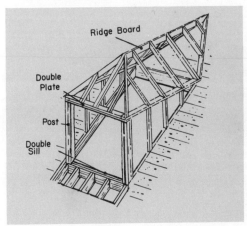

Ridge Board
Double Plate
Post
Double Sill

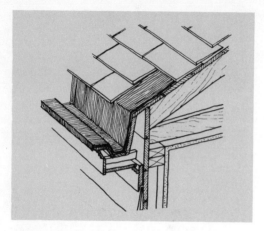

Ridge Cut—(See *Plumb cut*.)

Rise—The vertical distance through which anything rises, as the rise of a roof or stair.

Riser—The vertical board between two treads of a flight of stairs.

Roof—The covering or upper part of a building.

Roofing—The material put on a roof to make it wind and waterproof.

Run—The length of the horizontal projection of a piece such as a rafter when in position.

Saddle board—The finish of the ridge of a pitch-roof house. Sometimes called comb board.

Sash—The framework which holds the glass in a window.

Sawing, plain—Lumber sawed regardless of the grain, the log sim-

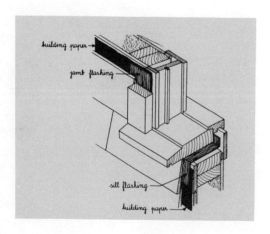

ply squared and sawed to the desired thickness; sometimes called slash or bastard sawed.

Scaffolding or staging—A temporary structure or platform enabling workmen to reach high places.

Scale—A short measurement used as a proportionate part of a larger dimension. The scale of a drawing is expressed as $\frac{1}{4}'' = 1$ foot.

Scantling—Lumber with a cross section ranging from $2''x4''$ to $4''x4''$.

Scarfing—A joint between two pieces of wood which allows them to be spliced lengthwise.

Scotia—A hollow molding used as a part of a cornice, and often under the nosing of a stair tread.

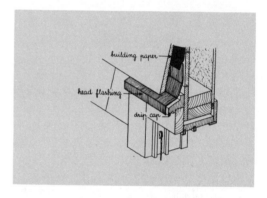

Scribing—The marking of a piece of wood to provide for the fitting of one of its surfaces to the irregular surface of another.

Seat cut or plate cut—The cut at the bottom end of a rafter to allow it to fit upon the plate.

Seat of a rafter—The horizontal cut upon the bottom end of a rafter which rests upon the top of the plate.

Section—A drawing showing the kind, arrangement, and proportions of the various parts of a structure. It is assumed that the structure is cut by a plane, and the section is the view gained by looking in one direction.

Shakes—Imperfections in timber caused during the growth of the tree by high winds or imperfect conditions of growth.

Sheathing — Wallboards, roofing boards; generally applied to narrow boards laid with a space between them, according to the length of a shingle exposed to weather.

Sheathing paper—The paper used under siding or shingles to insulate the house; building papers.

Siding—The outside finish between the casings.

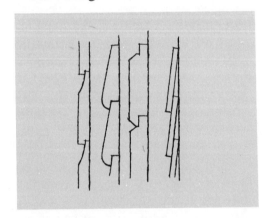

Sills—The horizontal timbers of a house which either rest upon the masonry foundations or, in the absence of such, form the foundations.

Sizing—Working material to the desired size; a coating of glue, shellac, or other substance applied to a surface to prepare it for painting or other method of finish.

Sleeper—A timber laid on the ground to support a floor joist.

Span—The distance between the bearings of a timber or arch.

Specifications — The written or printed directions regarding the

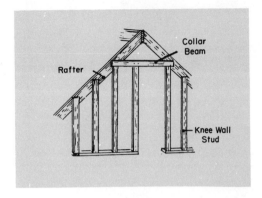

details of a building or other construction.

Square—A tool used by mechanics to obtain accuracy; a term applied to a surface including 100 square feet.

Stairs, box—Those built between walls, and usually with no support except the wall strings.

Standing finish—Term applied to the finish of the openings and the base, and all other finish necessary for the inside of the house.

Stucco—A fine plaster used for interior decoration and fine work, also for rough outside wall coverings.

Studding—The framework of a partition or the wall of a house; usually referred to as 2x4's.

Threshold—The beveled piece over which the door swings; sometimes called a carpet strip.

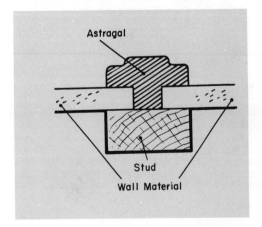

Timber—Lumber with cross section over 4″x6″, such as posts, sills and girders.

Tie beam (collar beam)—A beam so situated that it ties the principal rafters of a roof together and prevents them from thrusting the plate out of line.

Tin shingle—A small piece of tin

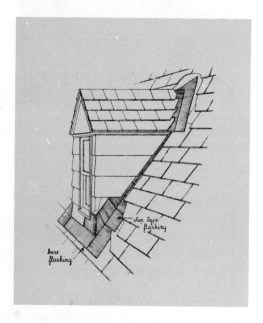

used in flashing and repairing a shingle roof.

To the weather—A term applied to the projecting of shingles or siding beyond the course above.

Tread—The horizontal part of a step.

Trim—A term sometimes applied to outside or interior finished woodwork and the finish around openings.

Trimmer—The beam or floor joist into which a header is framed.

Trimming—Putting the inside and outside finish and hardware upon a building.

Valley—The internal angle formed by the two slopes of a roof.

Verge boards—The boards which serve as the eaves finish on the gable end of a building.

Vestibule—An entrance to a house; usually inclosed.

Wainscoting—Matched boarding or panel work covering the lower portion of a wall.

Wash—The slant upon a sill, capping, etc., to allow the water to run off easily.

Water table—The finish at the bottom of a house which carries the water away from the foundation.

Wind ("i" pronounced as in kind)—A term used to describe the surface of a board when twisted (winding) or when resting upon two diagonally opposite corners, if laid upon a perfectly flat surface.

Wooden brick—Piece of seasoned wood, made the size of a brick, and laid where it is necessary to provide a nailing space in masonry walls.

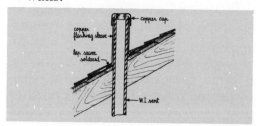

Grade

This architectural term refers to the level of the ground around a building.

Grain

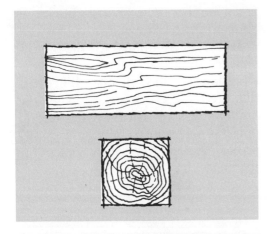

In woodworking, this refers to the direction of the wood fibers. When working on a piece of wood longitudinally, you may be working with or against the grain. When working transversely, you are working cross grain.

Graphite

Carbon, either natural or artificial, can be used as a lubricant. It can be purchased in powdered form or in a colloidal solution, and used to lubricate hinges, moving metal parts and, in particular, cylinder locks.

Grass

For a guide to the selection of the proper type of grass seed, see *LAWNS*.

Grease Trap

A grease trap is installed in a drainage system for the purpose of separating grease from waste water so that large quantities of grease are not discharged into the sewer. Grease traps are not used in the average household, but in some communities, grease traps or catch basins are required by law. With a septic tank, it is best to use a grease trap so as to avoid difficulties with the tank.

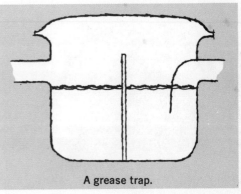

A grease trap.

Green Lumber

Timber from which the sap has not been removed either by natural seasoning or by kiln drying is called green lumber. As this wood dries, it tends to shrink and warp.

It is not economical for the handyman to use green lumber in any construction because of the difficulties that are bound to arise later when the lumber ages or dries. It is better to purchase seasoned lumber for any project except temporary braces or shoring.

Grindstone

Generally made of natural sandstone, a grindstone comes in the shape of a wheel. It is used for sharpening tools and for abrading metal which has rough edges or surface.

Also see *SHARPENING*.

Here a grindstone is attached to the saw arbor and used with a homemade jig to sharpen a chisel.

Photograph courtesy of DeWalt, Inc.

Grommet

These metal fittings are used to reinforce holes in fabric, such as awnings, which are laced to a framework. Grommets come in various sizes and types.

One type of grommet, see accompanying photograph, is set through a hole punched in the fabric and the end is peened over with a special grommet tool.

Another type of grommet is shaped like the one in the photograph, but a special metal ring is set over the male end on the opposite side of the fabric. When the end is peened over, it is forced over this ring. This makes a more secure fitting.

Groove

A groove is frequently called a dado. Actually, a groove is a cut along the edge of the wood.
Also see *DADO*.

Groove Joint Pliers

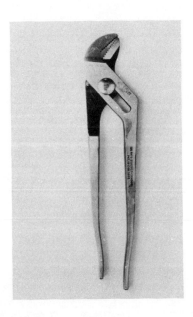

Also known as a parrot-head or pump pliers, the groove joint pliers have adjustable jaws with serrated edges. It is possible to grip varying sizes of nuts, bolts and other parts with this type of pliers. In an emergency, this type of pliers can also be used to hold smaller diameter pipe. The groove joint pliers come in several different sizes which determine the maximum opening of the jaws.

Ground Covers

If you wish to use ground covers around the exterior of the house, you will find suggestions for your selections in the section on *LANDSCAPING*.

Grounding, Tools and Appliances

Whether it be for the power tools of your workshop, or the household appliances such as the washing machine, or the television set, a necessary safety measure is proper grounding. This actually means forming an electrical connection to the ground, or earth, to save you from receiving a shock should you come into contact with an exposed wire in the house.

The grounding causes the fuse to blow; this in turn cuts off the electric power immediately, and thus you are

Grounding portable electric tools is usually done by attaching the "pigtail" to a special type of screw which is set in the cover plate of the receptacle. This technique works with BX cable and with Romex if the cable has a third wire properly connected throughout to ground the system.

rescued from the "live" current and any minor or severe shock you might otherwise undergo.

Method of Grounding

Grounding is done with a single electrical wire. The first step is to loosen a bolt on the appliance or tool. Then scrape the insulating covering off the end of the grounding wire, and insert this end under the bolt by turning it a couple of times. Next, tighten the bolt again. If any rust or dirt is on the metal surface or bolt, clean it off thoroughly before retightening the bolt.

The other end of the wire (the grounding end) is connected to a metallic electric cable or to a water pipe. In order to do this, you use a grounding clamp. You can buy such clamps at an electrical supply or hardware store; they have a bolt or some other device to tighten the ground end of the wire to the pipe, also a screw for making the wire secure.

Should you not have a pipe near the appliance or the power tools, you can accomplish the grounding by turning the end of the wire (the insulating covering scraped off the tip) over a screw which is on the plate of the outlet where your electrical appliance or tool is now plugged in. This presupposes, of course, that the wiring system of your home is properly grounded throughout.

Portable Electric Tools

The shock hazard may be greater

The newer power-tool cords come with a special three-prong plug made to fit a special receptacle. In this way, you automatically ground the tool whenever you connect it. There is no possibility that a pigtail will be left unconnected.

with portable tools, as they are sometimes used in damp places or outdoors.

Many of the newest models have an ordinary 2-prong plug, with no apparent grounding facility. These will often be found to bear identification that they are "double-insulated" and require no grounding for safety. Most other tools not so equipped will come with a 3-prong plug at the end of the power cord. This must be used with a properly grounded socket, if full protection is to be had. If no such socket is at hand, an adapter may be used instead, but the tool will not be safe unless the extra wire on the adapter is attached to a ground—usually the screw on the socket cover plate.

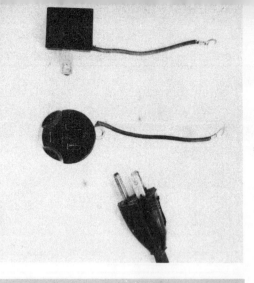

If your new power tool comes with the special three-prong plug and you want to use it in an outlet without the special receptacle, there is an attachment you can buy which plugs into the outlet. The extra wire is attached to the screw holding the cover plate on the outlet box.

Grout

This is a mixture of Portland cement, lime and sand with sufficient water to make a consistency that will flow easily without the separation of the ingredients. It is used to fill the spaces between ceramic and other types of tiles used on walls or floors. When combined with gravel it can also be used in setting posts for fences, filling voids or holes in concrete blocks when building regulations require solid masonry construction.

Gutters and Downspouts

It has been estimated that 5,000 gallons of water fall on the roof of the average house in this country during a year. Running down the sides of the house, this water will leave black streaks. Seeping through the brickwork, framing or masonry, it will rot the beams and ruin the interior walls. Striking the ground, it will dig holes in flower beds and gather in the basement.

The only real protection is a system of gutters and downspouts.

The gutters are made of wood, galvanized metal, aluminum or copper. While the latter two are generally more expensive than the others they require less maintenance and wear longer.

Basic Parts

In the accompanying illustration are a number of downspouts, gutters and fittings. If you examine your roof, you will undoubtedly find many of these used.

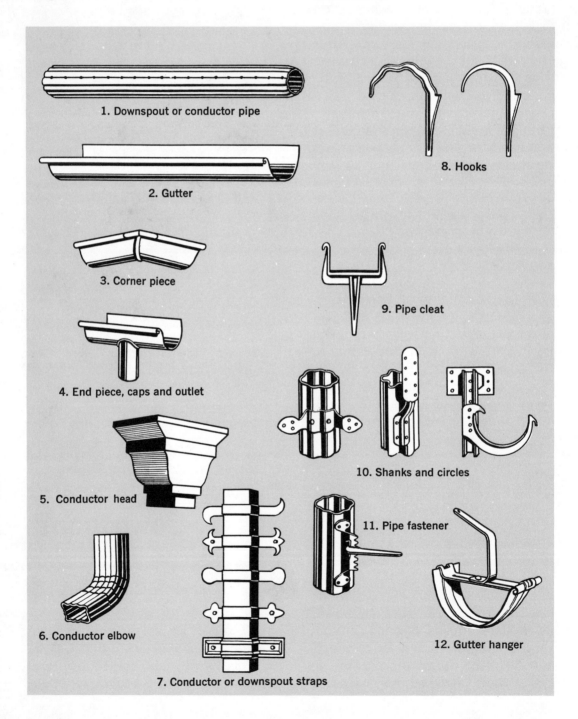

1. Downspout or conductor pipe

2. Gutter

3. Corner piece

4. End piece, caps and outlet

5. Conductor head

6. Conductor elbow

7. Conductor or downspout straps

8. Hooks

9. Pipe cleat

10. Shanks and circles

11. Pipe fastener

12. Gutter hanger

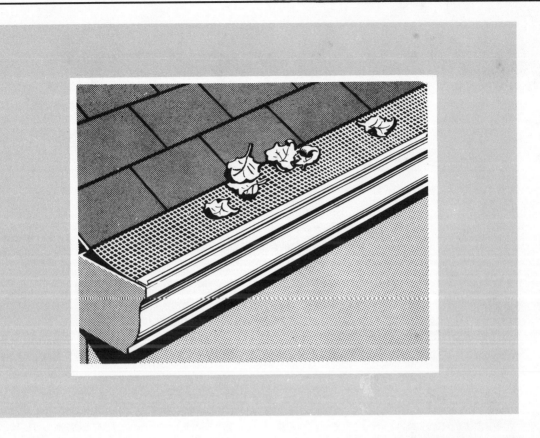

Keeping Gutters Clean

Difficulty may arise from the accumulation of leaves, rubbish, and birds' nests in gutters. Such debris, if not promptly removed, may stop up the opening to the downspout and cause water to back up and flow over the edge. This overflow may cause considerable damage if the gutters are built into the cornice, for water can find its way down inside the walls of the house. Unsightly streaks and stains on the exterior wall surfaces may also result if the overflow is not stopped.

To prevent leaves and other refuse from being washed into the downspout, it is advisable to place a basketlike strainer over the gutter outlet. Strainers are usually kept in stock by hardware dealers and are inexpensive. Even when there is no stoppage or overflow, it is advisable to keep gutters clean, because rotting leaves will eventually cause the metal to corrode and leak if allowed to remain. Fine ash and dirt should be removed regularly, as cinders in contact with metal will set up a corrosive action. When dirt of this kind is removed, the gutter should be flushed with clean water to remove all traces of acid.

These conditions may be avoided if the householder will remember to clean out the gutters regularly, especially in the autumn after the leaves have fallen.

It is also advisable to remove unusually heavy snow and ice from gutters to aid roof drainage and prevent damage to gutters or their

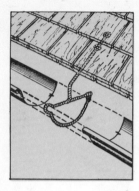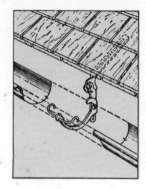

Typical gutter hangers.

fastenings by the excessive weight of such masses. The life of downspouts and metal gutters may be extended considerably by painting them occasionally with good metal paint.

Repairing Metal Gutters

Metal gutters may be half-round or shaped like a cornice but repairs are similar for both types. To correct a buckle or fold in the metal it may be necessary to remove the gutter. The crease can then be hammered out with a soft-faced hammer and a block of wood shaped like the gutter. The hammer head should be of wood, fiber, or plastic to keep it from marring the surface of the gutter.

Small holes may be repaired with a drop of solder and large ones patched with a piece of sheet metal of the same kind as the gutter. The metal must have a clean bright finish or the solder will not adhere. A temporary patch may be made with a piece of roofing felt or cotton duck fastened with flashing cement. The patching material should be thoroughly clean and dry, and both sides of the patch should be given a liberal but even coating of cement.

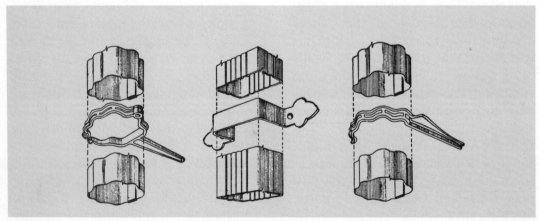

Typical downspout fasteners.

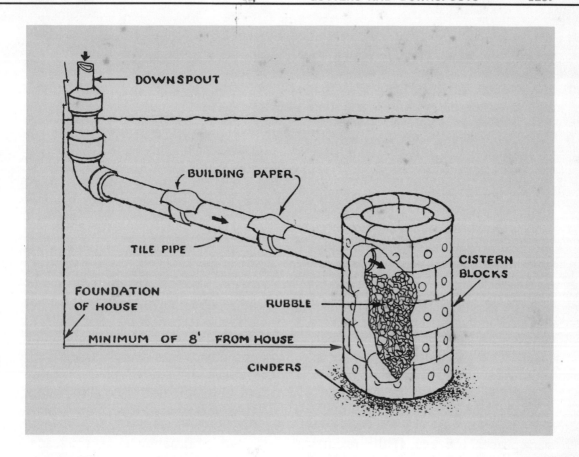

Repairing Wood Gutters

If a one-piece molded wood gutter has sagged, it should be forced back into place with a heavy hammer and block of wood and renailed in the proper position. Nails should be set, holes puttied, and unpainted spots touched up. The trough may then be treated with linseed oil or given a coat of asphalt paint.

If there is a split in a wood gutter, it can be repaired by patching with sheet metal. Coated iron, copper, or aluminum sheets can be used. Galvanized iron nails should be used for iron sheets, copper nails for copper sheets, and aluminum nails for aluminum sheets.

The metal should be shaped to fit the gutter and should be wide enough to cover the inside surface of the gutter and the tops of both edges. The area to be patched should be thoroughly cleaned, painted with asphalt paint, and covered with a layer of flashing cement, applied with a putty knife. The metal patch should then be pressed into the cement, nailed at intervals of 1½″ along all edges, and another coat of cement applied to seal the edges, cover the nail holes, and protect the metal. If patches are over 10″ in length, additional lines of nails should be used, spaced about 8″ between lines.

The lining of box or trough-type gutters, that is, wood lined with metal, should be examined for cracking. When ice forms in a gutter trough which is deep and narrow, it may expand and force the wall of the trough to loosen or break and the metal to split. For this reason, shallow and wide box gutters are advisable since they permit ice to expand over the edge of the gutter without injuring the box. Box-type gutters should be lined with rustproof metal. If other metal is used, the inside of the gutter should be swabbed with bituminous material or painted with metal paint.

Repairing Gutter Hangers

Metal gutters are attached to the eaves by means of straps of sheet metal, long spikes, twisted wire rope, or adjustable or nonadjustable metal brackets. These hangers may break or pull loose from their fastenings, permitting the gutter to sag and prevent proper drainage. If this occurs, broken straps or hangers should be replaced and adjusted so that the gutter will slope downward with a uniform grade to the outlet end. If supports are too far apart, it may be necessary to install additional hangers to insure a uniform slope for the gutter.

Downspouts (or Leaders)

Downspouts require less attention than gutters, but a certain amount of upkeep is necessary. Slush working down into pipe elbows may freeze, forcing seams and folds to open and allow water to leak through or drip. A leak is more common where leaders are not corrugated to allow for expansion. When a leak starts it should be checked promptly; otherwise the defect may increase until the whole elbow is broken. Recurrent freezing and thawing of a metal leader tube that fills with water because of stoppage may cause it to split. Small splits or bulges can be pressed back into shape and soldered. However, if a downspout is badly broken or rusted, it may be necessary to replace the entire section. The method of removal will depend upon the type of fastening used. The leader pipe comes in sections which fit into each other. To insert a length of pipe, the upper section should be slipped into the lower so that water will flow on the inside and not leak out. To make the installation more secure the sections should be soldered together at the joints.

Also see *DRY WELL*.

Guy Rope

While any rope or wire used for bracing against the wind is called a guy wire or guy rope, technically, a guy rope is a galvanized rope. It consists of 6 strands of 7 wires each with a hemp core.